Bus

Bus

✓

Carpentry: Tools
Shelves·Walls·Doors

Cy DeCosse Incorporated
Minnetonka, Minnesota

Contents

Introduction **5**

CY DECOSSE INCORPORATED

A COWLES MAGAZINES COMPANY

Chairman/CEO: Bruce Barnet
Chairman Emeritus: Cy DeCosse
President/COO: Nino Tarantino
Executive V.P./Editor-in-Chief:
 William B. Jones

CARPENTRY: TOOLS • SHELVES • WALLS •
DOORS

Created by: The Editors of Cy DeCosse
Incorporated, in cooperation with Black
& Decker. Black & Decker is a trademark of Black & Decker (US), Incorporated
and is used under license.

Also available from the publisher:
*Everyday Home Repairs, Decorating With
Paint & Wallcovering, Kitchen Remodeling,
Building Decks, Home Plumbing Projects &
Repairs, Basic Wiring & Electrical
Repairs, Workshop Tips & Techniques,*
*Advanced Home Wiring, Carpentry:
Remodeling, Landscape Design &
Construction, Bathroom Remodeling,
Built-in Projects for the Home*

Library of Congress
Cataloging-in-Publication Data

Carpentry: Tools • Shelves • Walls • Doors

(Black & Decker home improvement library)
Includes index. 1. Carpentry - Amateurs'
manuals.
I. Series.

TH5607.C36 1989 694 88-23718

ISBN 0-86573-704-5
ISBN 0-86573-705-3 (Pbk.)

Project Directors: Gary D. Branson,
  John Riha
Senior Art Director: Tim J. Himsel
Art Director: Barbara Falk
Editor: Bryan Trandem
Project Manager: Barbara Lund
Production Manager: Jim Bindas
Assistant Production Manager:
  Julie Churchill
Production Staff: Russell Beaver, Janice
  Cauley, Holly Clements, Sheila DiPaola, Joe
  Fahey, Kevin D. Frakes, Yelena Konrardy,
  Scott Lamoureux, Bob Lynch, Jody Phillips,
  Linda Schloegel, Nik Wogstad

Shop Director: Greg Wallace
Set Builder: Andrew Dahl
Studio Manager: Cathleen Shannon
Staff Photographers: Bobbette Destiche,
  Rex Irmen, Tony Kubat, John Lauenstein,
  Bill Lindner, Mark Macemon, Mette Nielsen
Contributing Photographers: Rudy Calin,
  Paul Englund, Jim Erickson, Stefano
  Grisci, Chuck Nields, Steve Olson,
  Richard Wiseman
Copy Editor: Barb Machowski
Contributing Individuals and Agencies: Will
  and Merrilee Lotzow, American Plywood
  Association, Western Wood Products
  Association

Contributing Manufacturers: American Brush
  Company, Inc.; Cooper Industries
  (including registered trademarks:
  Crescent, Lufkin, Nicholson, Plumb,
  Turner, Weller, Wire-Wrap, Wiss, Xcelite);
  Muralo/Elder Jenks; The Stanley Works;
  United Gilsonite Laboratories; USG Corp.;
  Yale Security, Inc.
Printed on American paper by:
  R. R. Donnelley & Sons Co. (0495)

Introduction

Understanding carpentry is an important first step for many home improvement and repair projects. With basic carpentry skills and the correct tools, you can easily accomplish a wide variety of tasks around the home. In the process you'll be twice rewarded: you'll save money by doing the work, and you'll enjoy the sense of accomplishment that comes from completing the job yourself.

Carpentry: Tools·Shelves·Walls·Doors is intended for the home owner who would like to learn about basic carpentry. Written with clear, nontechnical language and completely illustrated with color photographs, this book will introduce you to essential tools and guide you, step by step, through common repair and home improvement projects. We've taken special care to include tips from industry professionals that will help you complete your projects safely and precisely.

The first section, *Tools*, will help you select a set of basic carpentry tools you will need for the home. With these essential tools, you'll be able to measure, cut, drill, pry, smooth, and shape in a variety of materials. In addition to providing purchase recommendations and information about basic tool techniques, this section includes an introduction to lumber and plywood, and explains how these and other building materials can best be used to suit your home carpentry needs.

You'll also learn about nails, screws, and adhesives. Finally, organize your workspace and prepare for home projects by building our heavy-duty workbench and sawhorses. Our step-by-step instructions show you how.

Subsequent chapters have been devoted to common home carpentry projects that will encourage you to put your skills to work. Build shelves, construct interior walls, fit wooden trim and moldings, and hang and repair doors. Large color photographs let you see each part of the process completely before you even begin.

Do-it-yourself home improvement projects can provide a great sense of satisfaction. *Carpentry: Tools·Shelves·Walls·Doors* will allow you to complete these projects safely and successfully, and will help you enjoy your home to the fullest.

Tools & Materials

Framing square

C-clamp

16-oz. claw hammer

Phillips screwdriver

Standard screwdriver

Plumb bob/
chalk line

Nail
sets

Mallet

Sanding
block

2' carpenter's level

Putty
knife

Chisel

Utility
knife

Electronic
stud
finder

⅜'' power
drill

Drill bits

Combination
square

T-bevel

Cordless
screwdriver

Cat's
paw

12' tape
measure

Wonderbar®

Crosscut
saw

Wallboard
saw

Starter tool set should include a generous selection of hand tools, plus a ⅜-inch power drill and a cordless screwdriver. Inspect the finish on hand tools. Quality hand tools made of high-carbon steel are machined with clean-cut metal surfaces. Tool handles should be tight and comfortably molded.

Tool Basics

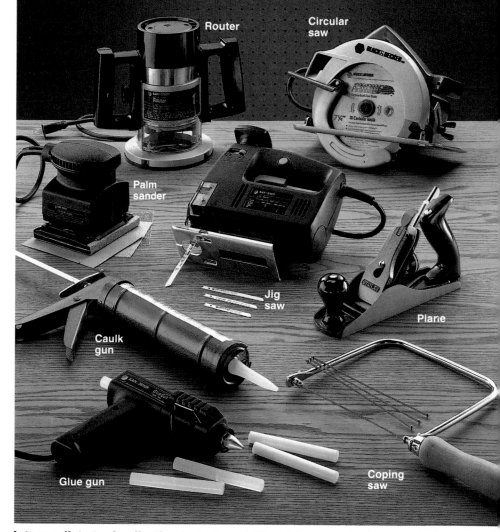

A quality tool collection does not require a large initial investment. A home owner can build a tool collection by buying tools as they are needed for each carpentry project. Invest in top-grade tools made by reputable manufacturers. A quality tool always carries a full parts and labor warranty.

Read power tool specifications to compare features like horsepower, motor speed and cutting capacity. Better-quality tools also have roller or ball bearings instead of sleeve bearings, reinforced power cords, and heavy-duty trigger switches.

Intermediate tool collection includes additional power tools and special-purpose hand tools. Replace blades or resharpen cutting tools whenever they become dull.

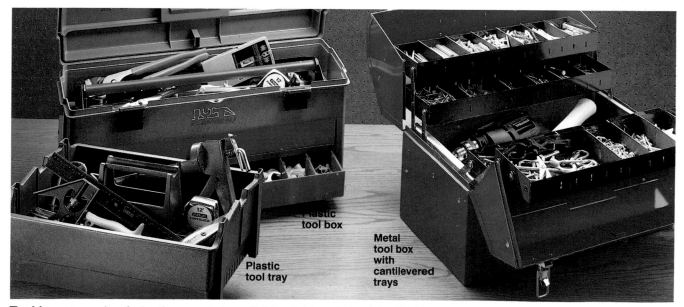

Tool boxes made of plastic or metal are lightweight and durable. Tool boxes with cantilevered trays and divided compartments keep tools and materials organized.

Measuring & Layout Tools

An important first step in every carpentry project is measuring distances and angles accurately. Buy a steel tape measure with a ¾-inch-wide blade for general home use.

A combination square is a compact tool used to measure and mark 45° and 90° angles. Use a framing square to lay out 90° angles. Choose a T-bevel with a locking handle to measure and transfer any angle.

To check surfaces for plumb and level, buy a quality 2-foot carpenter's level made of metal or wood. Select a level with screw-in bubble vials that can be replaced if they are damaged. Also buy a string chalk line to lay out long, straight lines.

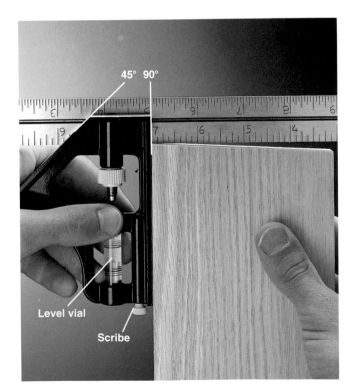

Steel tape measure with ¾-inch-wide blade is good for general-purpose home use. Choose a tape with blade marked every 16" for easy layout of stud or joist locations.

Combination square is many tools in one. The adjustable handle has two straight surfaces for marking 90° and 45° angles. The square also has a built-in level. Some squares include a pointed metal scribe to mark work for cutting.

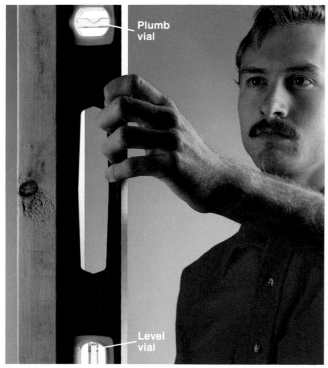

Two-foot carpenter's level has plumb vial for checking vertical surfaces and a level vial for checking horizontal surfaces. Level shows correct position when bubble is exactly between the line markings.

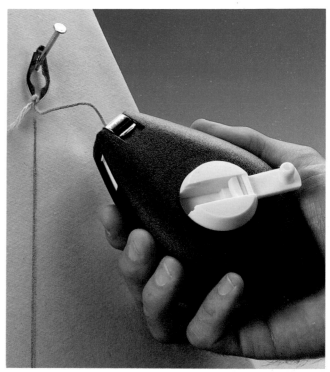

Chalk line marks long lines needed for large layout jobs. Hold string taut at both ends, and snap firmly to mark surface. Chalk line can also be used as a plumb bob for laying out stud walls (pages 84-87).

How to Duplicate Angles with a T-bevel

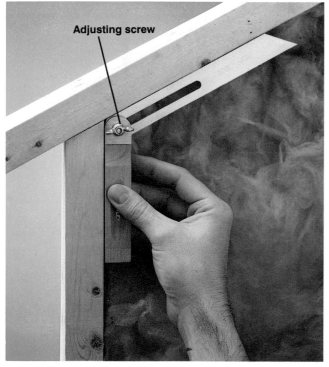

1 Loosen the T-bevel adjusting screw and adjust the arms to match the angle to be copied. Tighten the adjusting screw.

2 Move the T-bevel to the workpiece, and mark the profile of the angle. Cut the workpiece to match the angle.

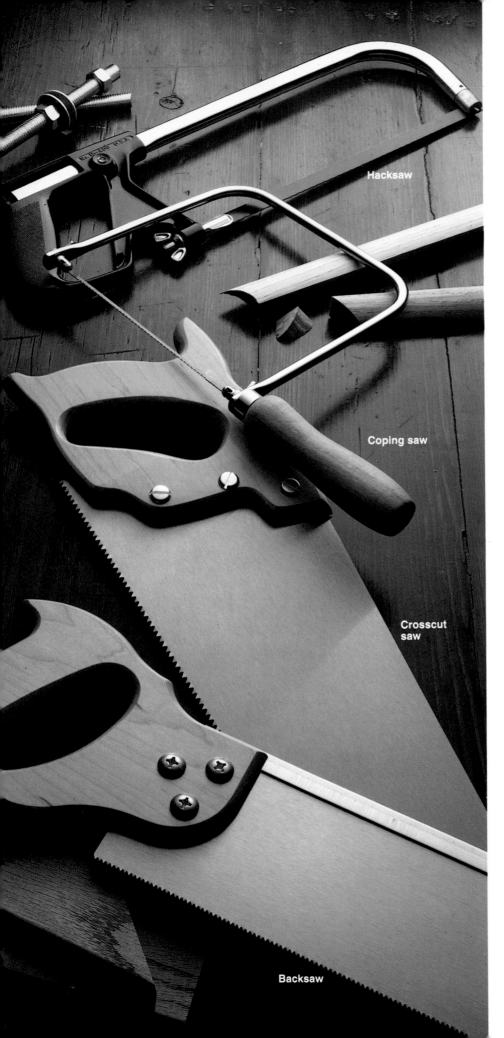

Hacksaw

Coping saw

Crosscut saw

Backsaw

Handsaws

Handsaws can be more practical than portable power saws for small jobs and occasional use.

The crosscut saw is a standard cutting tool designed to cut across the wood grain. A crosscut saw may also be used for occasional "rip" cuts parallel to the wood grain. A crosscut saw with 10 teeth per inch is a good choice for general-purpose cutting.

A backsaw and miter box makes straight cuts. The reinforced spine keeps the backsaw blade from flexing. The miter box locks at any angle for cutting precise miters and bevels.

A coping saw makes curved cuts on materials like wood molding. The coping saw has a very narrow, flexible blade held taut by a C-shaped spring frame. To adjust blade position for scroll cuts, rotate the spigots holding the blade.

Hacksaws are designed to cut metal. Like a coping saw, a hacksaw has a fine, flexible blade that can be replaced when it becomes dull.

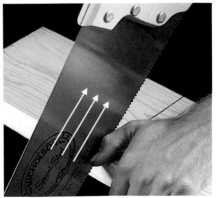

Begin handsaw cuts with upward strokes to establish the cut line, then make long, smooth strokes with blade at 45° angle to workpiece. Guide the saw at the beginning of a cut by supporting the edge with the side of your thumb.

Crosscut saw is a standard carpenter's tool. At end of cut, saw slowly and support waste material with a free hand to prevent the wood from splintering.

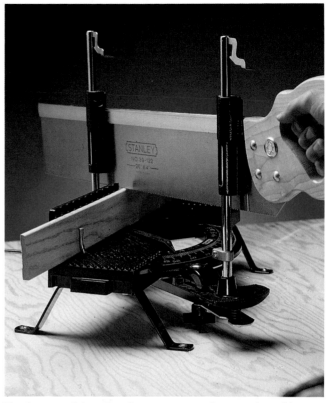

Backsaw with miter box cuts precise angles. Clamp or hold workpiece in miter box. Make certain that miter box is securely fastened to work surface.

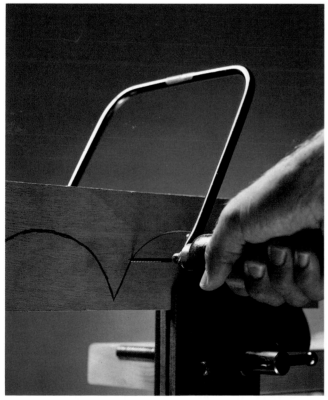

Coping saw has a thin, flexible blade designed to cut curves. It is a necessary tool for cutting and fitting wood moldings.

Hacksaw has a flexible, fine-tooth blade designed to cut metal. Blade must be stretched tightly in frame.

Circular Saw

The power circular saw is ideal for making fast, straight cuts in wood. Special-purpose saw blades make it possible to cut metal, plaster or even concrete with a circular saw. The locking baseplate pivots to adjust blade depth, and rotates for bevel cuts.

Choose a saw with blade size of at least 7¼ inches. A smaller saw may not cut through 2-inch lumber, especially when set at a bevel position. Select a saw with a motor rated at 2 horsepower or more.

Because a circular saw blade cuts as it rotates upward, the top face of the workpiece may splinter. To protect the finished side of the workpiece, mark measurements on back side of workpiece. Place the good side down, or facing away from the baseplate, when cutting.

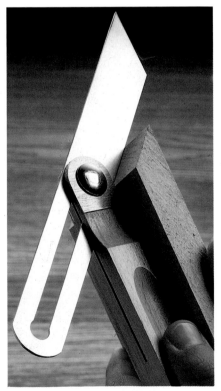

Check the cutting angle of circular saw with a T-bevel or square. Make test cuts on scrap wood. If bevel scale is inaccurate, adjust the baseplate to compensate (page opposite).

Use an edge guide for straight, long cuts. Clamp a straightedge on the workpiece. Keep baseplate tight against edge guide and move the saw smoothly.

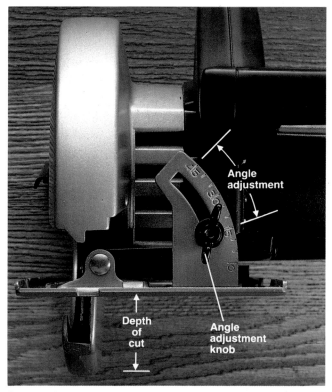

Set blade angle by loosening the adjustment knob. Set blade depth by loosening adjustment knob at rear of saw. For safety, set the blade so that it projects through bottom of workpiece by no more than the length of one saw tooth. Tighten knobs firmly.

Circular saw blades include: carbide-tipped combination blade for general use; panel blade with small teeth which do not chip thin veneer layers in plywood; hollow-ground planer blade with tapered surface that reduces friction, used for fine woodworking; abrasive blades used to cut metal or masonry.

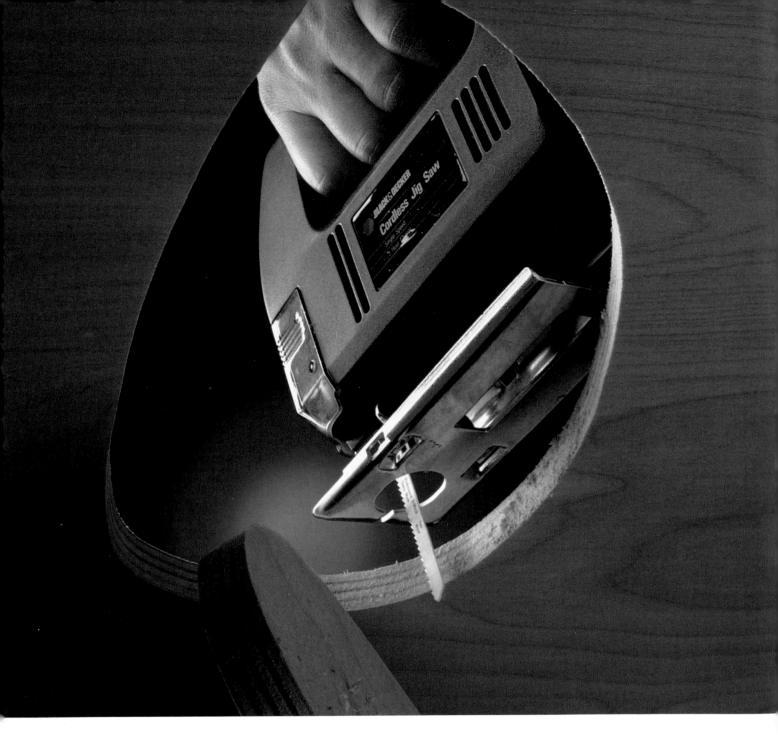

Jig Saw

The jig saw is the best choice for cutting curves. The cutting capacity of a jig saw depends on its power and the length of its blade stroke. Choose a saw rated to cut 2-inch-thick softwood and ¾-inch-thick hardwood stock. Some jig saws have a pivoting baseplate that can be locked to make bevel cuts.

Select a variable-speed jig saw, because different blade styles may require different cutting speeds for best results. In general, use faster blade speeds when cutting with coarse-tooth blades and slower speeds with fine-tooth blades.

A jig saw tends to vibrate because of the up-and-down blade action. A quality jig saw has a heavy-gauge steel baseplate that reduces vibration. To further minimize vibration, hold the saw tightly against the workpiece, and move the saw slowly so the blade does not bend.

Because jig saw blades cut on the upward stroke, the top side of the workpiece may splinter. If the wood has a good side to protect, cut with this surface facing downward.

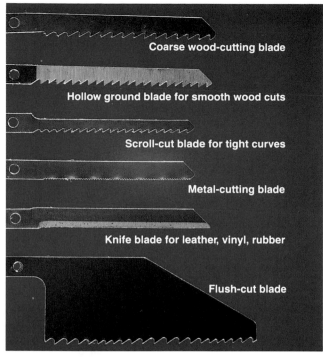

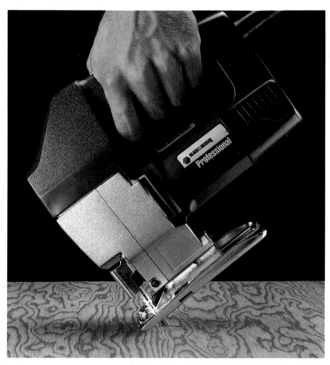

Jig saw blades come in different designs for cutting different materials. Choose a blade that is correct for the job. With fine-tooth blades that have 14 or more teeth per inch, set saw at low blade speed. Coarse blades require faster blade speeds.

Plunge cuts are made by tipping the saw so front edge of the baseplate is held firmly against workpiece. Start saw, and slowly lower it to a horizontal position, letting blade gradually cut through workpiece.

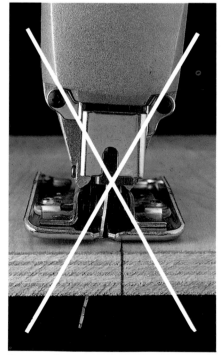

Scroll or curved cuts are made with a narrow blade. Move saw slowly to avoid bending the blade. Some jig saws have a scrolling knob that allows the blade to be turned without turning the saw.

Cut metals with a fine-tooth metal-cutting blade and select a slow blade speed. Support sheet metals with thin plywood to eliminate vibration. Use emery paper or a file to smooth burred edges left by jig saw blade.

Do not force blades. Jig saw blades are flexible and may break if forced. Move saw slowly when cutting bevels or tough materials like knots in wood.

Hammers

Hammers are made in a wide variety of sizes and shapes. Choose a hammer with a smoothly finished, high-carbon steel head and a quality handle made of hickory, fiberglass, or solid steel.

The 16-ounce curved claw hammer is the most frequently used hammer for carpentry. It is designed only for driving, setting, or pulling nails. For all other striking jobs, use a specialty hammer. A tack hammer with a magnetic head drives nails and tacks that are too small to hold. A rubber- or plastic-head mallet drives wood chisels. Select a ball peen hammer to pound hardened metal tools, like masonry chisels or pry bars, because it has a heat-treated steel head that resists chipping.

Use a nail set to drive nail heads below the work surface without damaging the wood.

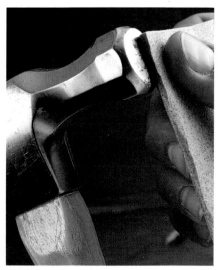

Clean hammer face periodically with fine sandpaper. Wood resins and nail coatings may build up on the face, causing the hammer to slip and mar the work surface or bend the nail.

Tack hammer

Rubber-head mallet

Ball peen hammer

Claw hammer

Nail set

Hammering Tips

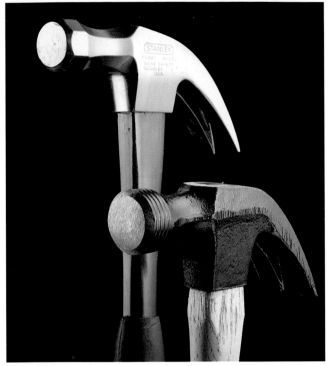

Claw hammer drives and pulls nails. Choose a quality hammer (left) with a 16-ounce head. Look for a smoothly finished, high-carbon steel head. Bargain tool (right) has rougher, painted finish with visible cast marks.

Tack hammer with magnetic head drives small nails or brads that are difficult to hold by hand.

Mallet with rubber or plastic head drives woodworking chisels. Soft mallet face will not damage fine woodworking tools.

Ball peen hammer has heat-treated steel head that resists chipping when driving hardened steel tools or pry bars.

Nail set drives heads of finish and casing nails below wood surface. Choose a nail set with tip that is slightly smaller than nail head.

Nails

The wide variety of nail styles and sizes makes it possible to choose exactly the right fastener for the job. Use either common or box nails for general framing work. Box nails are smaller in diameter, which makes them less likely to split wood. Most common and box nails have a cement or vinyl coating that improves their holding power.

Finish and casing nails have small heads and are driven just below the work surface with a nail set, for projects like nailing wood trim. Casing nails have a slightly larger head than finish nails for better holding power. Galvanized nails have a zinc coating that resists rusting, and are used for outdoor projects.

Other specialty nails are identified by their intended function, like wallboard nails, siding nails, masonry nails, or flooring nails.

Nail lengths are identified by numbers from 4 to 60 followed by the letter "d," which stands for "penny." Some specialty nails are identified by either length or gauge.

Nail Sizes

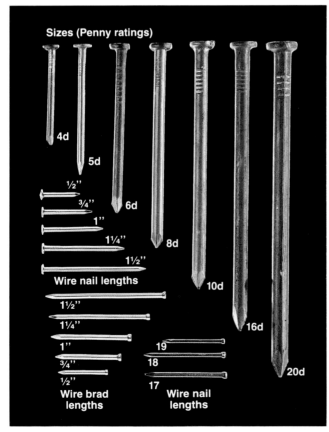

Sizes (Penny ratings)

4d
5d
6d
8d
10d
16d
20d

½"
¾"
1"
1¼"
1½"
Wire nail lengths

1½"
1¼"
1"
¾"
½"
Wire brad lengths

19
18
17
Wire nail lengths

Types of Nails

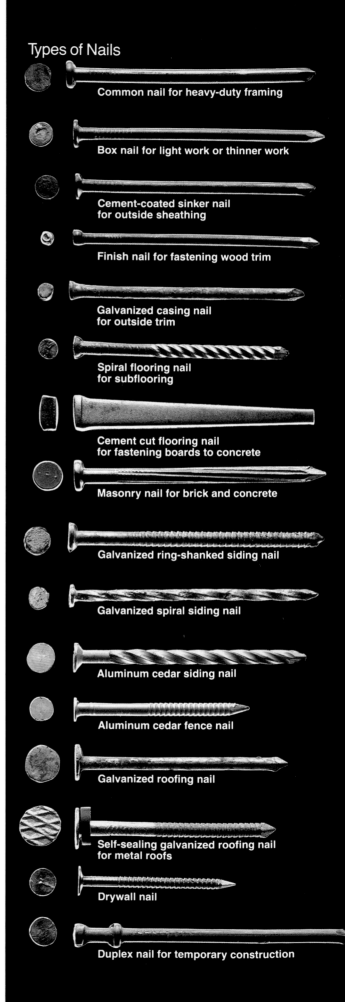

Common nail for heavy-duty framing

Box nail for light work or thinner work

Cement-coated sinker nail for outside sheathing

Finish nail for fastening wood trim

Galvanized casing nail for outside trim

Spiral flooring nail for subflooring

Cement cut flooring nail for fastening boards to concrete

Masonry nail for brick and concrete

Galvanized ring-shanked siding nail

Galvanized spiral siding nail

Aluminum cedar siding nail

Aluminum cedar fence nail

Galvanized roofing nail

Self-sealing galvanized roofing nail for metal roofs

Drywall nail

Duplex nail for temporary construction

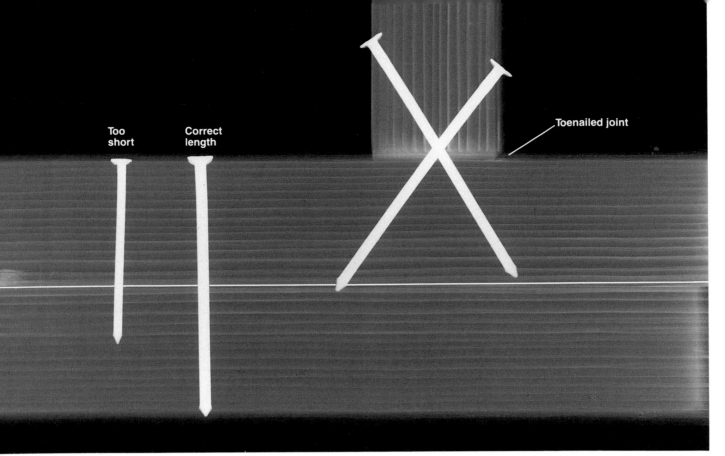

X-ray view shows how nails penetrate wood. Longer nail that fully penetrates second 2 × 4 has greater holding power than short nail. Use toenailing (right) when nails cannot be driven from the outside surface. Drive nails at opposing 45° angles. Offset nail positions so that nails do not hit each other.

Tips for Nailing

Drive flat concrete nails into the mortar joints instead of the concrete blocks. Mortar is easier to penetrate.

Metal connectors help join wood with ease and speed, and are often used to connect studs to sole and top plates.

How to Fasten Wood to a Steel Beam

1 Coat the top of 2 × 4 with a generous application of construction adhesive. Clamp 2 × 4 to bottom of I-beam.

2 Drill holes spaced 16″ on-center through 2 × 4 and base of I-beam, using ⁹⁄₆₄-inch twist bit. Use low speed when drilling metal. Drive 16d common nails through holes and clinch them on base of I-beam.

Clinch nails for extra holding power. Bend the nail over slightly, then drive it flush to the surface with a hammer.

Use finish nail in electric drill to bore a pilot hole in hardwood. Tighten drill chuck securely on nail.

Prying Tools

Quality pry bars are made of high-carbon steel, and are available in many sizes. Choose tools forged in a single piece. Tools made from welded parts are not as strong as those that are forged.

Most pry bars have a curved claw at one end for pulling nails and a chisel-shaped tip at the opposite end for other prying jobs. Improve leverage by placing a wood block under the head of pry tools.

Wonderbar® is a slightly flexible tool made of flattened steel. This tool is useful for a variety of prying and wrecking jobs. Both ends can be used for pulling nails.

Prying tools include wrecking bars for heavy demolition work, cat's paws for removing nails, and brad pullers. Wonderbars are made of flattened steel and come in a variety of sizes for light and heavy use.

Wrecking bar, sometimes called a crowbar, is a rigid, heavy-use tool for demolition and heavy prying jobs. Use scrap wood under the bar to protect surfaces.

Cat's paw has a sharpened claw. To extract nails, drive the claw into the wood under the nail head with a hammer.

Drills

Most drilling jobs can be done easily with a power drill. Power drills are commonly available in ¼-, ⅜- and ½-inch sizes. The number refers to the largest bit shank diameter that fits the drill chuck. A ⅜-inch drill is a good choice because it accepts a wide range of bits and accessories. A variable-speed reversing (VSR) drill will adapt to many uses, like drilling masonry, or driving and removing wallboard screws. A cordless drill offers freedom from extension cords.

When choosing a drill, look for quality features like an extra-long power cord with reinforced cord protector, and a sealed switch that prevents dirt from entering the trigger. A drill that uses top-quality materials may actually be smaller, lighter, and easier to handle than a cheaper drill.

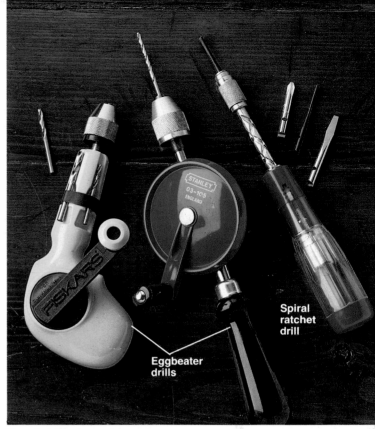

Spiral ratchet drill

Eggbeater drills

Hand drills include eggbeater and spiral ratchet styles. Hand drills are often used in fine woodworking, or for carpentry jobs where a power drill is not convenient.

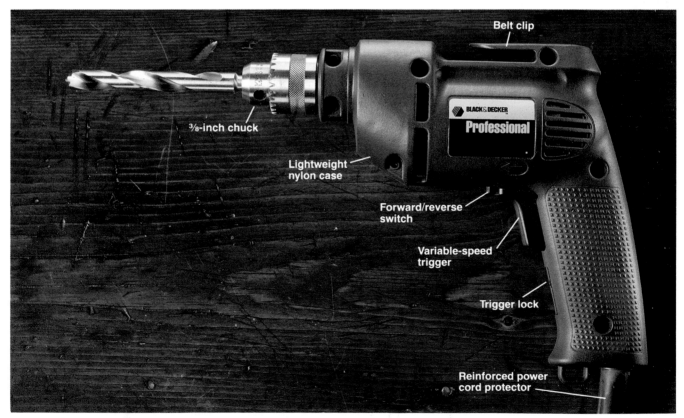

Belt clip

⅜-inch chuck

Lightweight nylon case

Forward/reverse switch

Variable-speed trigger

Trigger lock

Reinforced power cord protector

Power drill features to look for include ⅜-inch chuck size, variable motor speed, reversing feature, trigger lock to set a constant speed, a heavy power cord with reinforced protector, a tough lightweight nylon case, and a molded clip that allows the tool to be hung from a belt or pants pocket.

Drill Bits

Twist bits can be used to bore in both metal and wood. They come in many sizes, ranging from wire gauge to more than ½ inch wide. Some self-piloting bits have a special point for accurate drilling. Most twist bits are made from high-speed or carbon steel. For drilling stainless steel and other hard metals, choose a titanium or cobalt bit.

Spade bits have a long point and flat-edged cutters and are used to cut holes in wood quickly and accurately. Other types of drill bits are available for special applications, like drilling extra-large holes for a lockset, or boring into concrete. Store drill bits so they do not bump against each other, and clean them with linseed oil to prevent rust.

Twist bit can be used in wood or metal. Drill wood at high speeds, metal at low drill speeds.

Pilot tip

Self-piloting bit requires no center punch. Special tip reduces splintering in wood, and prevents bit from binding when drilling metal.

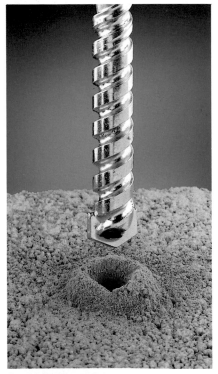

Carbide-tipped masonry bit can drill in concrete, cinder block or brickwork. Use low drill speed, and lubricate drill hole with water to prevent overheating.

Glass & tile bit drills smooth holes in smooth, brittle surfaces. Use low drill speed, and wear gloves and eye protection.

Drill saw has twist tip to cut entry hole, and side-cutting rasp teeth for reaming cuts in wood, plastic or light-gauge metals.

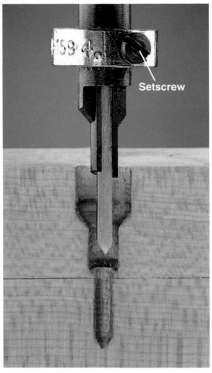

Spade bit is used to drill wood. Long tip anchors bit before the cutting edges enter the wood. Begin at low speed, gradually increasing as bit enters wood.

Adjustable counterbore bit drills screw pilot, countersink and counterbore holes with one action. Loosen setscrew to adjust bit to match length and shape of screw.

Plug cutter cuts circular wood plugs used to fill screw counterbore holes.

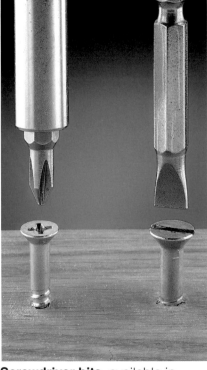

Hole saw with mandrel pilot bit cuts smooth holes in wood, like those used to mount door locksets.

Screwdriver bits, available in many styles, convert a variable-speed drill into a screwgun.

Extractor bit removes screws with worn or broken heads. Drill a pilot hole into top of screw with twist bit, then use extractor and reverse drill setting to remove screw.

Drilling Tips

Tap an indentation in wood or metal with a center punch. Starting point keeps drill bit from wandering.

Cover drilling area on glass or ceramic with masking tape. Tape keeps bit from wandering on smooth surface.

Use a backer board underneath workpiece to prevent splintering when drill bit breaks through.

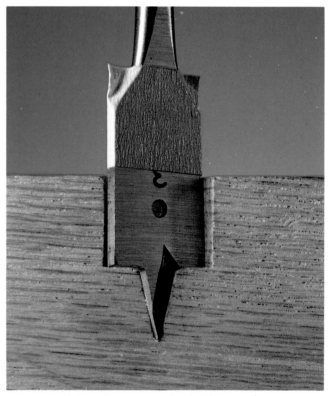

Wrap masking tape around drill bit to control depth of hole. Drill until bottom of tape is even with top of workpiece surface.

Lubricate metal with cutting oil while drilling. Oil prevents bit from overheating. Use low speed when drilling metal.

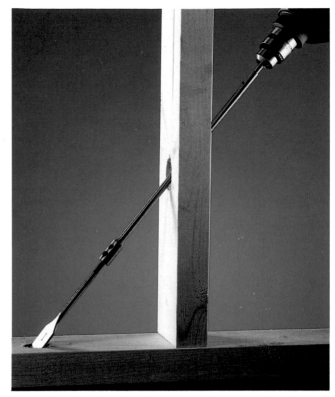

Use bit extension to drill deep or inaccessible holes. Drill at low speed until bit is fully engaged.

Prebore holes in hardwood and metal with a small bit. Preboring prevents bit from binding and wood from splintering.

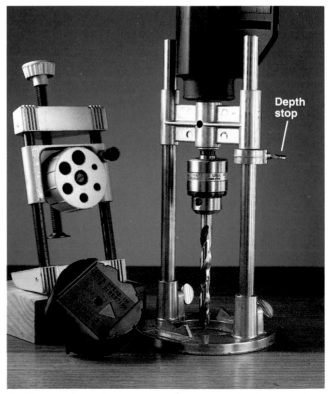

Depth stop

Guide accessories control drilling angles for precise perpendicular holes. Drill guide (right) has adjustable depth stop that controls drilling depth.

Screwdrivers & Screws

Make sure you have several hand screwdrivers, both phillips and slot types. Quality screwdrivers have hardened-steel blades and wide handles that are easy to grip.

For general use, a cordless power screwdriver saves time and effort. For frequent use, or for large jobs like installing wallboard panels, choose a power screwgun with an adjustable clutch to set screws at different depths.

Screws are categorized according to length, slot style, head shape and gauge. The thickness of the screw body is indicated by the gauge number, from 0 to 24. The larger the gauge number, the larger the screw. Large screws provide extra holding power, while small screws are less likely to split a workpiece. When joining two pieces of wood, choose a screw length so that the entire threaded portion will extend into base piece.

Where appearance is important, use countersink or counterbore bits to drill a recessed hole that will hide the screw head. A countersink bit lets you drive a flat-head screw flush with the wood surface, while a counterbore bit lets you recess the screw head to hide the location with a wood plug.

Common screwdrivers include (from top): stubby model for use in cramped areas, adjustable-clutch screwgun for fastening wallboard, ratchet hand screwdriver with interchangeable bits, cordless power screwdriver with locking spindle, slot screwdriver.

Types of screws: lag screw, galvanized utility screw, Grip-It® twist anchor screws, flat-head wood screws, pan-head sheetmetal screw, oval-head screw, hex-head sheetmetal screw, wallboard screw, flat-head phillips wood screw, hi-low screw.

Tips for Driving Screws

Lubricate screws with beeswax to make driving easier. Do not use soap, oil or grease to lubricate, because they can stain wood and corrode screws.

Pilot hole keeps wood from splitting when screw is driven. Use a twist bit with diameter that is slightly less than diameter of threaded portion of screw.

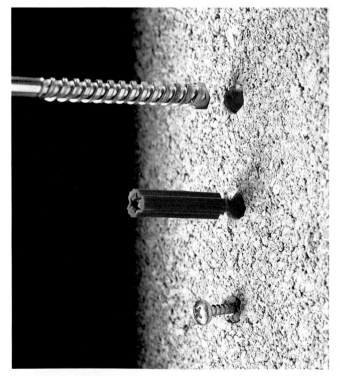

To install a wall anchor, drill a pilot hole in wall equal in diameter to plastic anchor. Insert anchor and drive it flush with wall. Inserted screw will expand anchor for strong, durable hold.

Use masonry & wall anchors for attaching to plaster, concrete or brick. Choose an anchor that is equal in length to the thickness of the wall surface.

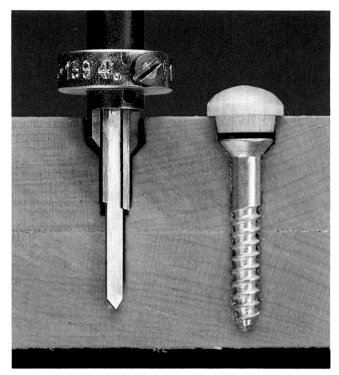

Drill counterbore pilot holes with adjustable counterbore bit. Loosen setscrew and set bit to match length and shape of wood screw. Tighten setscrew and drill until collar reaches surface of workpiece. After driving screw, cover hole with wood plug or putty.

Utility wallboard screws have wedge-shaped heads that are self-countersinking. Wallboard screws are designed so they will not split wood. Use black screws for inside jobs, and galvanized screws for exterior work.

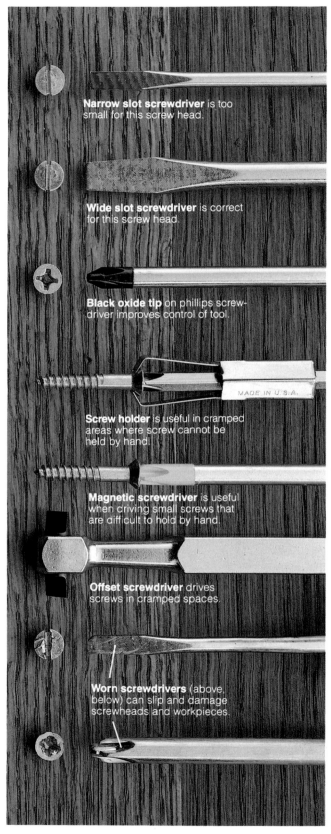

Narrow slot screwdriver is too small for this screw head.

Wide slot screwdriver is correct for this screw head.

Black oxide tip on phillips screwdriver improves control of tool.

Screw holder is useful in cramped areas where screw cannot be held by hand.

MADE IN U.S.A.

Magnetic screwdriver is useful when driving small screws that are difficult to hold by hand.

Offset screwdriver drives screws in cramped spaces.

Worn screwdrivers (above, below) can slip and damage screwheads and workpieces.

Choose proper screwdriver for the job. Screwdriver should fit slot tightly. Common types of screwdrivers include: slot, phillips, phillips with black oxide tip, screw holder, magnetic, and offset screwdrivers.

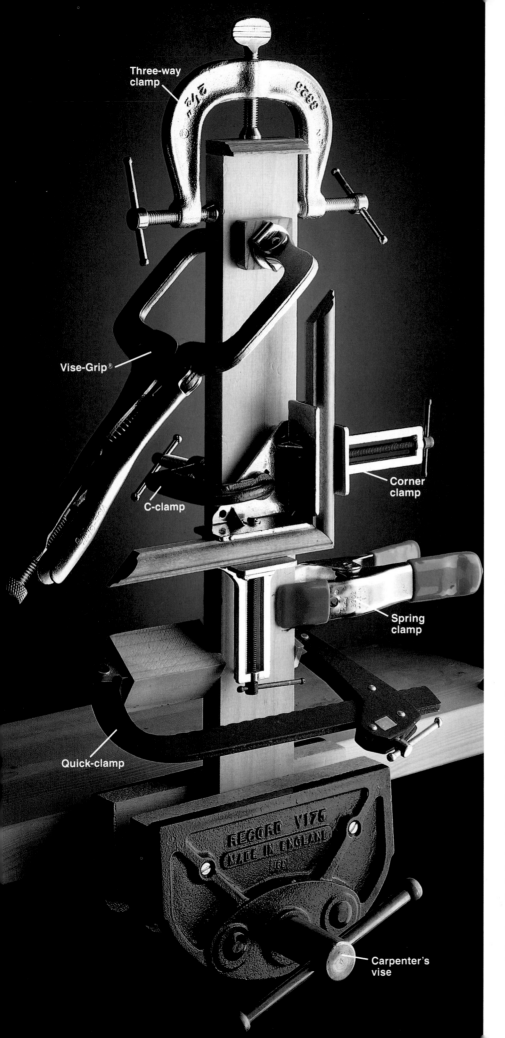

Three-way clamp

Vise-Grip®

C-clamp

Corner clamp

Spring clamp

Quick-clamp

Carpenter's vise

Clamps, Vises & Adhesives

Use vises and clamps to hold materials in place while working. Equip a workbench with a heavy-duty carpenter's vise. Clamps for small jobs include C-clamps, Vise-Grip® clamps, handscrews, and quick clamps. Clamps with metal jaws can damage a workpiece, so use scrap wood blocks between the workpiece and the clamp jaws.

For wide clamping jobs, use pipe clamps or bar clamps. The jaws of pipe clamps are connected by ordinary steel pipe. The distance between the jaws is limited only by the length of the pipe.

Adhesives bond many materials that cannot easily be nailed or screwed together, like concrete or steel. They also can reduce the number of fasteners needed to install wallboard or paneling. Many new adhesives are resistant to moisture and temperature changes, making them suitable for exterior use.

Common adhesives include (clockwise from top right): clear adhesive caulk for sealing cracks in damp areas, waterproof construction adhesive, multi-purpose adhesive, electric hot glue gun with glue sticks, yellow wood glue, white wood glue, and white all-purpose glue.

Joist & deck adhesive makes for a stronger, squeak-free floor or deck. Make sure that adhesive is waterproof for outdoor applications.

Carpenter's vise attaches to workbench to hold materials for cutting, shaping or sanding. Cover the broad jaws with hardwood to protect workpieces.

Electric hot glue gun melts glue sticks for both temporary and permanent bonding of wood and a variety of other materials.

Tips for Gluing & Clamping

Handscrews are wooden clamps with two adjusting screws. Handscrews are used to hold materials together while gluing. The wide wooden jaws will not damage workpiece surfaces. Handscrews adjust to fit angled workpieces.

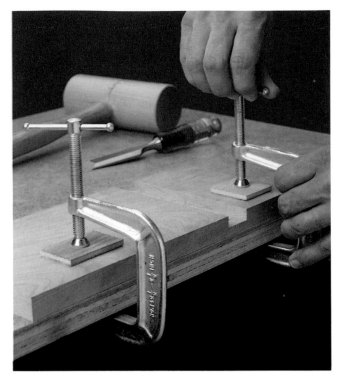

C-clamps range in clamping capacity from 1 to 6". To protect the workpiece, place scrap wood blocks between the jaws and the workpiece surface.

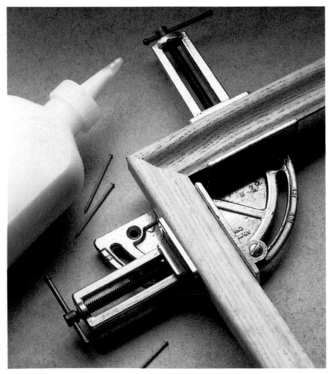

Corner clamp holds mitered corners when gluing picture frame moldings. Glue and clamp opposite corners, and let them dry before gluing the remaining corners.

Three-way clamp has three thumbscrews, and is used to hold edge moldings to the side of a shelf, tabletop or other flat surface. Use scraps of wood to protect workpiece surfaces.

Strap clamp and white carpenter's glue are used for gluing furniture and other wood projects. Use yellow glue for exterior projects. Clamp the pieces together until the glue dries.

Pipe clamps or bar clamps hold large workpieces. Buy pipe clamp jaws in pairs to fit either ½-inch or ¾-inch diameter pipe. Clamping irregular shapes may require clamping jigs made from scrap lumber.

Workmate® portable gripping bench has a jointed, adjustable table that tightens to clamp a workpiece. Accessories, like bench stops, increase the gripping bench's versatility.

Vise-Grip® clamps provide good holding power and are easily adjusted. The hand-grip closing action makes these clamps quicker to use than traditional C-clamps.

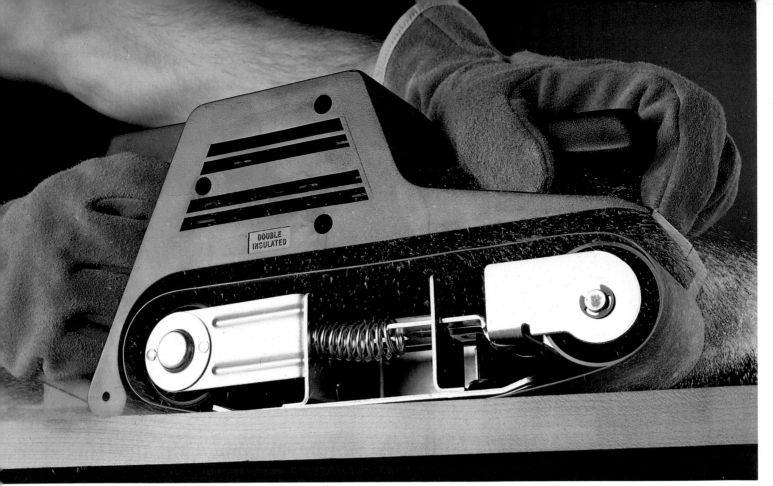

Sand large areas quickly with a belt sander. Disposable belts are available in grits ranging from 36 (extra-coarse) to 100 (fine).

Sanding

Power sanding tools and sandpaper shape and smooth wood and other building materials. For very large areas, like hardwood floors, use a high-speed floor belt sander. Portable belt sanders are suitable for most work involving rough, fast removal of material. Finishing sanders, sometimes called orbital sanders, are best for light to medium removal of material. For very small, intricate, or contoured areas, sand by hand with folded sandpaper or a sanding block.

Sanders come in several sizes and speed ranges. Small "quarter-sheet" sanders are compact and easy to handle. Larger "half-sheet" sanders are better for sanding large areas. High-speed sanders are best for removing large amounts of material, while lower-speed tools create a fine, smooth finish. Variable-speed sanders offer the greatest flexibility for different applications.

Sandpaper is available in a wide range of grits. The lower the grit number, the coarser the grit. Sanding is usually done in steps, proceeding from coarse-grit sandpaper to finer grits.

Hand sanding block is helpful for small surfaces. For curved areas, wrap sandpaper around a folded piece of scrap carpeting. Sandpaper conforms to shape of workpiece.

60-grit coarse sandpaper is used on hardwood flooring and to grind down badly scratched surfaces. Move sander across the grain for quickest removal.

100-grit medium sandpaper is best used for initial smoothing of wood. Move sander in direction of wood grain for smoothest surface.

150-grit fine sandpaper puts finish smoothness on wood surfaces. Use fine sandpaper to prepare wood surfaces for staining, or to smooth wallboard joints.

220-grit extra-fine sandpaper is used to smooth stained wood before varnishing, or between coats of varnish.

Quality finishing sanders have high-speed motors and orbital action, and can flush-sand in tight work areas. For rough-sanding, move tool across the wood grain. For smooth-finishing, move sander in same direction as wood grain.

Sanding accessories for power drills include (clockwise from top right): disc sander for fast sanding, sanding drums and flap sander to smooth contoured surfaces, and sanding drum on drill attachment.

Planes & Chisels

Shave and smooth wood with a hand plane. A hand plane has a flat cutting blade set in a steel base and is used to smooth rough surfaces or reduce the width of a piece of wood.

A wood chisel has a flat steel blade set in a handle. It cuts with light hand pressure, or by tapping the end of its handle with a mallet. A wood chisel is often used to cut hinge and lock mortises.

For best results with any shaping tool, make several shallow cuts instead of one deep cut. Forcing a tool to make deep cuts may ruin both the tool and the workpiece.

Before You Start:
Tip: For safety and ease of use, keep shaping tools sharp by honing them on an oilstone or waterstone. Choose a combination stone that has both a coarse and fine face. The stone must be soaked in water or light oil to prevent damage to the tempered metal.

How to Plane a Rough Edge

Heel

Toe

Clamp workpiece into vise. Operate plane so wood grain runs "uphill" ahead of plane. Grip toe knob and handle firmly, and plane with long, smooth strokes. To prevent dipping (overplaning at beginning and end of board), press down on toe of plane at beginning of stroke, and bear down on heel at end of stroke.

How to Chisel a Mortise

1 Mark outline of mortise with pencil. For strike-plate mortises on door frames, or for hinge mortises, use hardware as marking template when drawing outline.

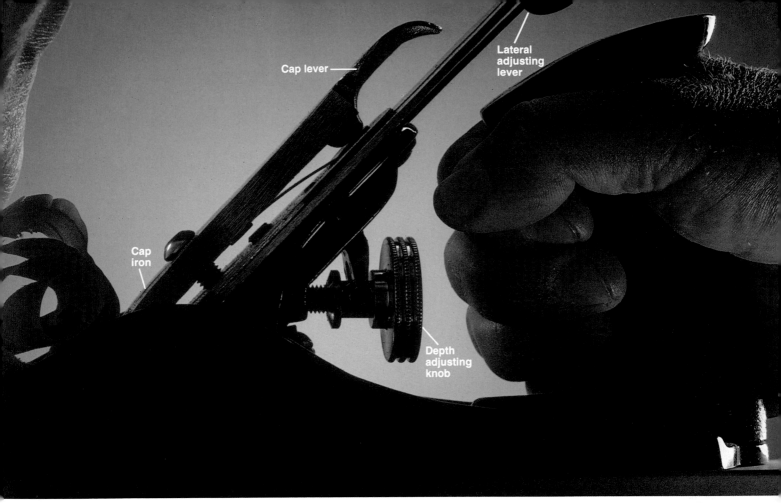

Set plane blade depth with adjusting knob. Properly set cutter will remove wood shavings that are paper-thin. Plane may jam or gouge wood if cutter is set too deep. Use lateral adjusting lever to align cutter for an even cut. If edge of cutter leaves a score mark on wood, check lateral adjustment. Loosen the cap lever to set the cap iron 1/16'' back from tip of blade.

2 Cut outline of mortise. Hold chisel with bevel-side in, and tap butt end lightly with mallet until cut is at proper depth.

3 Make a series of parallel depth cuts 1/4'' apart across mortise, with chisel held at 45° angle. Drive chisel with light mallet blows to butt end of chisel.

4 Lever out waste chips by holding chisel at a low angle with bevel-side toward work surface. Drive chisel by light hand pressure.

Router

Cut decorative shapes, make grooves, and trim laminates with a router. A router is a high-speed power tool that uses changeable bits to perform a variety of cutting and shaping tasks. Because a router runs at speeds up to 25,000 revolutions per minute, it can make very smooth cuts in even the hardest woods.

For best results, make a series of routing passes, gradually extending the bit until cut reaches the correct depth. Experiment to find the proper speed for moving the router. Pushing the tool too fast slows the motor, causing the wood to chip and splinter. Moving it too slowly can scorch the wood.

Choose a router with a motor rated at 1 horsepower or more. Safety features may include a conveniently placed ON/OFF trigger switch, clear plastic chip guard, and a built-in work light.

Tip: Router bits spin in a clockwise direction, so the tool has a tendency to drift to the left. For best control, feed the router from left to right so that the cutting edge of the bit feeds into the wood.

Decorative edging is usually made with a bit that has a pilot at the tip. The round pilot rides against the edge of the workpiece to control the cut.

Common Router Bits

Corner rounding bit makes simple finish edges on furniture and wood moldings.

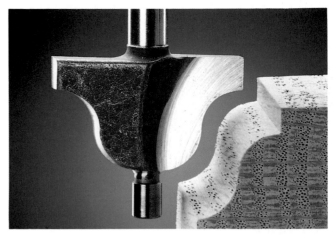

Ogee bit cuts a traditional, decorative shape in wood. Ogee bits are often used to create wood moldings and to shape the edges of furniture components.

Rabbet bit makes step-cut edges. Rabbeted edges are often used for woodworking joints and for picture frame moldings.

Laminate trimmer bit cuts a finished edge on plastic laminate installations. Ball-bearing pilot prevents bit from scorching face of laminate.

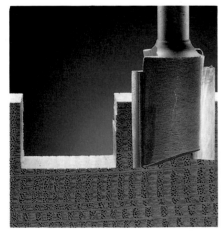

Straight bit cuts a square, flat-bottomed groove. Use it to make woodworking joints, or for free-hand routing.

Dovetail bit cuts wedge-shaped grooves used to make interlocking joints for furniture construction and cabinetwork.

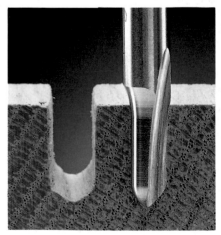

Veining bit is a round-bottomed cutter used for free-hand decorative carving and lettering.

Accessories

A few common accessories can make your work quicker and easier. A tabletop bench grinder with abrasive wheels helps clean and sharpen tools. A tool belt with pockets keeps tools and materials handy. An extension cord with multiple receptacles extends the mobility of your power tools.

A small portable tool table can make a jig saw or router more convenient to use. The tool table lets you securely mount a router or jig saw upside down, and has an adjustable edge fence and a miter guide to improve the accuracy of the tools.

Bench grinder accepts different abrasive wheels for grinding, polishing, or sharpening tools. Keep eye shields in place and wear additional eye protection when using bench grinder.

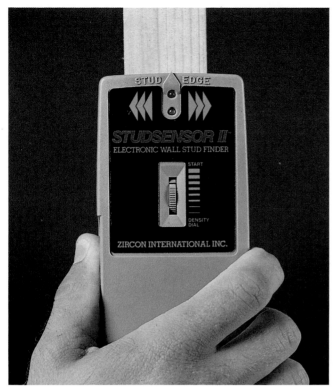

Electronic stud finder detects studs inside wall, and pinpoints both edges of the framing member. Red light comes on when the tool senses changes in wall density caused by underlying stud.

Multi-receptacle extension cord lets you plug in several power tools at the same location. To prevent electrical shock, use an extension cord that has a ground-fault circuit interrupter (GFCI).

Tool belt with pockets and hammer hook keeps nails, screws and small tools handy. Wide, web belt is most comfortable for extended wear.

Portable tool table makes a jig saw or router more stable. The adjustable edge fence improves control of shaping cuts. Make sure tool table is held firmly to tabletop or workbench.

Hammer drill combines impact action with rotary motion for quick boring in concrete and masonry. To minimize dust and to keep bits from overheating, lubricate the drill site with water. A hammer drill can also be used for conventional drilling when the motor is set for rotary action only.

Tools for Special Jobs

For one-time jobs or large projects, you may be able to rent or borrow special tools to make the work easier. For example, to frame a room addition or storage shed, rent an air-powered nailer that sinks framing nails with a squeeze of the trigger. Tool rental costs only a few dollars an hour, and can save hours of effort.

If you regularly work on a variety of home carpentry projects, consider buying additional power tools. For the home remodeler, a reciprocating saw is often useful. For fine woodworking and finish carpentry, a power miter box cuts angles quickly and accurately. For all-around carpentry and frequent use, invest in a table saw.

Stud driver fires a small gunpowder charge that propels masonry nails into concrete or brick. Use a stud driver to anchor a sole plate to a concrete floor.

Table saw and other stationary power tools provide greater capacity and accuracy for frequent carpentry and woodworking projects.

Power miter box cuts trim molding quickly and accurately. Locking motor assembly rotates up to 47° in both directions.

Air-powered nailer or stapler is attached to an air compressor. Tool trigger releases a burst of air to drive nails or staples into wood.

Reciprocating saw can be used for making cutouts in walls or floors, where a circular saw will not work, or for cutting metals like cast-iron plumbing pipes.

Check lumber visually before using it. Stored lumber can warp from temperature and humidity changes.

Lumber

Lumber for construction is usually milled from strong softwoods and is categorized by grade, moisture content, and dimension.

Grade: Characteristics such as knots, splits, and slope of the grain affect the strength of the lumber and determine the grade.

Lumber Grading Chart

Grade	Description, uses
SEL STR or select structural 1,2,3	Good appearance, strength and stiffness. 1,2,3 grades indicate knot size
CONST or Construction STAND or Standard	Both grades used for general framing, good strength and serviceability
STUD or Stud	Special designation used in any stud application, including load-bearing walls
UTIL or Utility	Used for economy in blocking and bracing

Moisture content: Lumber is also categorized by moisture content. S-DRY (surfaced dry) is the designation for lumber with a moisture content of 19% or less. S-DRY lumber is the least likely to warp or shrink and is a good choice for framing walls. S-GRN (surfaced green) means the lumber contains a moisture content of 19% or more.

Exterior lumber: Lumber milled from redwood or cedar is naturally resistant to decay and insect attack, and makes a good choice for exterior applications. The most durable part of a tree is the heartwood, so specify heartwood for wood that will be in contact with the ground.

Lumber injected with chemicals under pressure is resistant to decay. Pressure-treated lumber is generally less expensive than redwood or cedar. For outdoor structures like decks, use pressure-treated

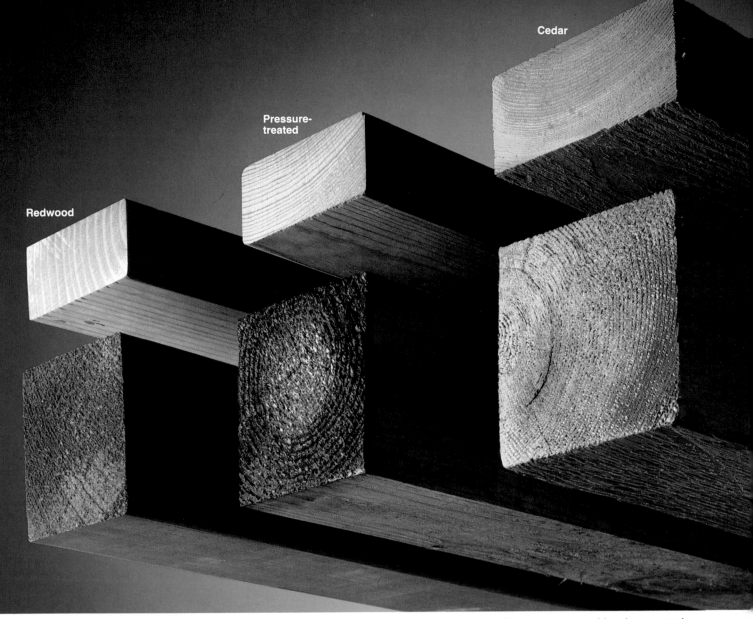

Redwood

Pressure-treated

Cedar

Build longer-lasting outdoor structures by using redwood, pressure-treated lumber or cedar. Redwood and cedar are more attractive, but pressure-treated lumber is less expensive. All are available in common lumber for posts and joists, and more attractive redwood or cedar for decks and railings.

Dimension: Lumber is sold according to nominal sizes common throughout the industry, such as 2 × 4 and 2 × 6. The actual size of the lumber is smaller than the nominal size.

lumber dimensions. Pressure-treated lumber contains toxic chemicals, so wear gloves and a protective particle mask when working with these products.

How to Read Lumber Markings

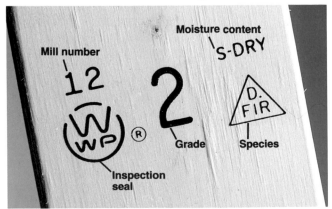

Check grade stamp on lumber for grade, moisture content and species.

Nominal vs. Actual Lumber Dimensions

Nominal	Actual
1 × 4	¾" × 3½"
1 × 6	¾" × 5½"
1 × 8	¾" × 7½"
2 × 4	1½" × 3½"
2 × 6	1½" × 5½"
2 × 8	1½" × 7½"

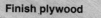
Finish plywood

Sheathing plywood

Strandboard

Particleboard with
plastic laminate

Waferboard

Particleboard

Plywood & Sheet Goods

Plywood is a versatile building material made by laminating thin layers or "plies" of wood together and forming them into panels. Plywood is available in thicknesses ranging from 3/16 to 3/4 inch.

Plywood is graded A through D, according to the quality of the wood used on its outer plies. It is also graded for interior or exterior usage. Plywood is classified by group numbers, based on the wood species used for the face and back veneers. Group 1 species are the strongest and stiffest, Group 2 the next strongest.

Finish plywood may have a quality wood veneer on one side and a utility-grade ply on the other side. This will be graded A-C. If it has a quality veneer on *both* sides, the grade will be A-A.

Sheathing plywood is for structural use. It may have large knotholes that make it unsuitable for finish purposes. Sheathing plywood is rated for thickness, and is graded C-D with two rough sides. Sheathing plywood has a waterproof bond. Plywood rated EXPOSURE 1 is for use where some moisture is present. Plywood rated EXTERIOR is used in applications that are permanently exposed to weather. Sheathing plywood also carries a thickness rating and a roof and floor span index, which

How to Read Finish Plywood Markings

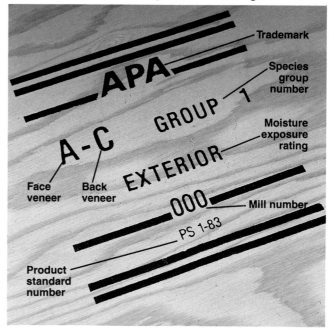

Trademark

Species group number

Moisture exposure rating

Mill number

APA

GROUP 1

A-C

EXTERIOR

000

PS 1-83

Face veneer

Back veneer

Product standard number

Finish plywood grading stamp shows the grade of face and back veneers, species group number, and a moisture exposure rating. Mill numbers and product numbers are for manufacturer's use.

appear as two numbers separated by a diagonal slash. The first number, for roofing applications, indicates the widest allowable spacing for rafters. The second number indicates the widest spacing for joists when plywood is used for subflooring.

Strand-, particle-, and waferboards are made from waste chips or inexpensive wood species.

Plastic laminates, like Formica®, are durable, attractive surfaces for countertops and furniture. Particleboard is strong and dimensionally stable, making it an ideal base for plastic laminates.

Plastic foam insulating board is light in weight and provides good insulation for basement walls.

Water-resistant wallboard is made for use in high-moisture areas, like behind ceramic wall tiles.

Wallboard, also known as drywall, Sheetrock®, and plasterboard, comes in panels 4 feet wide by 8, 10, or 12 feet long, and in 3/8-, 1/2-, and 5/8-inch thicknesses.

Pegboards and hardboards like Masonite® are made from wood fibers and resins bonded together under high pressure.

How to Read Sheathing Plywood Markings

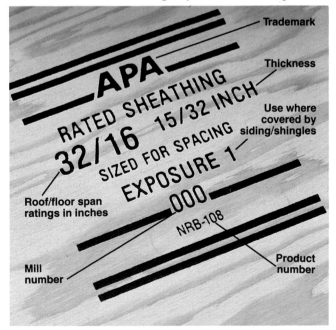

Trademark

Thickness

APA
RATED SHEATHING
32/16 15/32 INCH
SIZED FOR SPACING
EXPOSURE 1
000
NRB-108

Use where covered by siding/shingles

Roof/floor span ratings in inches

Mill number

Product number

Sheathing plywood grading stamp shows thickness, roof or floor span index and exposure rating, in addition to manufacturer's information.

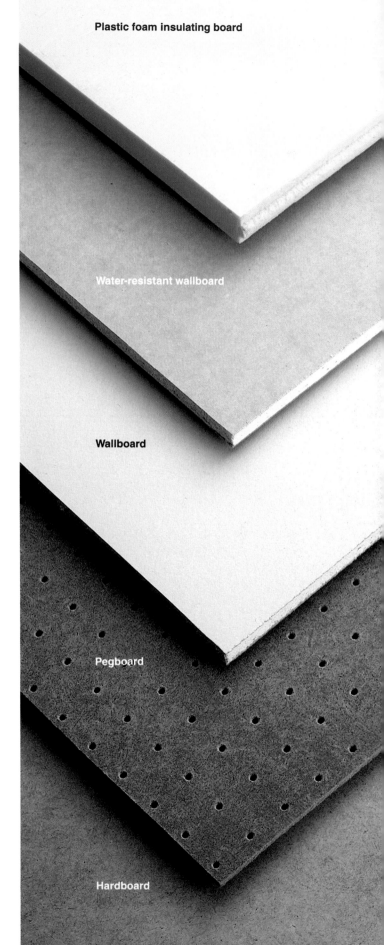

Plastic foam insulating board

Water-resistant wallboard

Wallboard

Pegboard

Hardboard

The Work Area

A good work area is well lighted with 4-foot fluorescent shop lights. The workshop should have an adequate electrical supply, and should have sturdy shelving for storing materials and tools.

Isolate your work area from living areas, so shop noises and debris will not disturb others. Also, work far away from a forced-air furnace, so that dirt or fumes cannot be sucked into the furnace and circulated through the house.

Store hand tools conveniently by mounting a pegboard hanger above your workbench.

Before You Start:
Tools & Materials for Pegboard Tool Hanger:
hot glue gun, metal washers, screwgun and wallboard screws (for stud walls), or power drill with masonry bits (for concrete walls), pegboard.

How to Build a Pegboard Tool Hanger

Finish washer

1 Use a hot glue gun to attach metal washers over peg holes on back side of pegboard. Space washers across pegboard to match spacing of wall studs (every 16 or 24"). Washers hold pegboard out from wall so tool hooks may be inserted.

2 Position pegboard on wall so that holes backed by washers are over stud locations. Drive wallboard screws through pegboard and washers into studs. Use finish washers if desired. For concrete walls, attach pegboard with masonry anchors (page 34).

Tips for Hanging Tools

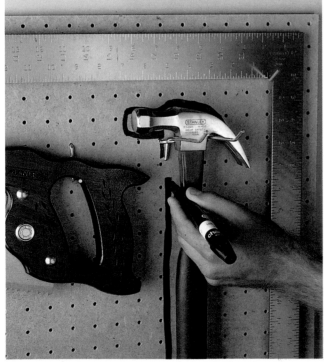

Trace tools with felt-tip pen so that they can be returned to the same location after use.

Glue hangers to pegboard with hot glue gun to prevent them from falling out when tools are removed.

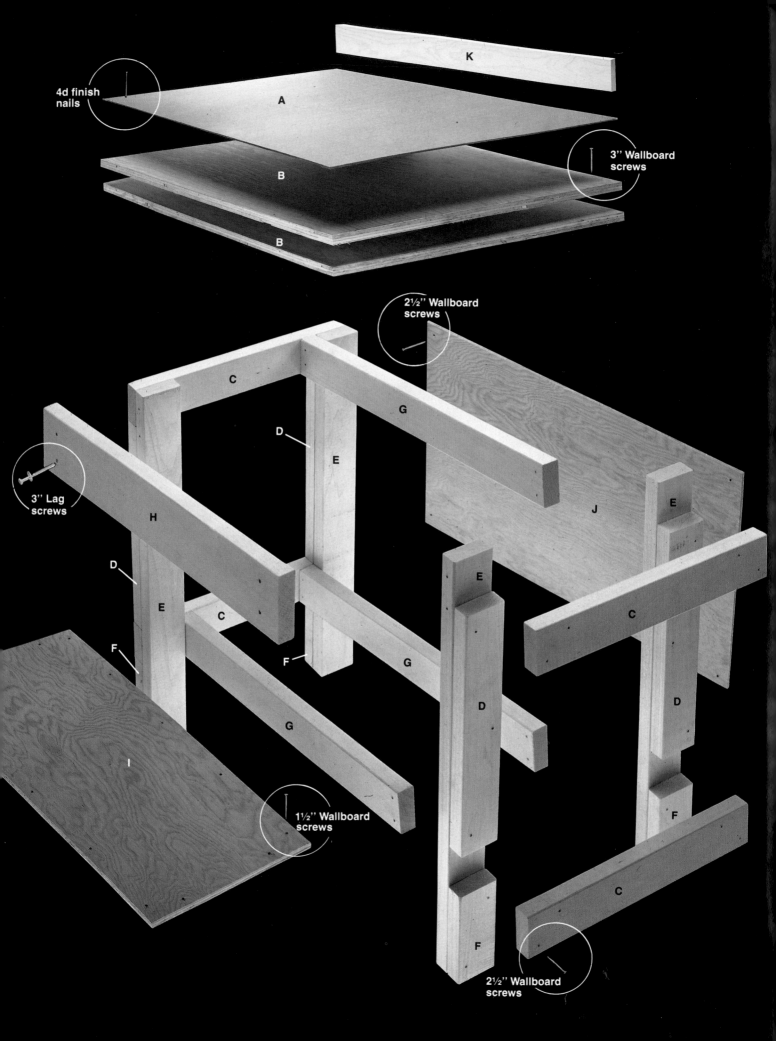

4d finish
nails

K

A

3'' Wallboard
screws

B

B

2½'' Wallboard
screws

C

D

G

E

3'' Lag
screws

H

J

E

D

E

C

E

C

F

D

F

G

D

G

I

F

1½'' Wallboard
screws

F

C

F

2½'' Wallboard
screws

Building a Workbench

This workbench has heavy-duty legs to support big loads, and a sturdy double-layer top to withstand pounding. Cover the top with a hardboard surface that can be removed when it becomes damaged. Build a shelf below the work surface for storing power tools. If desired, mount an all-purpose vise bolted to the front or top of the workbench.

Before You Start:

Tools & Materials: circular saw, carpenter's square, wallboard screws (1½-, 2½-, and 3-inch), screwgun or cordless screwdriver, drill and bits, lag screws (1½- and 3-inch), ratchet or adjustable wrench, 4d finish nails, nail set.

Tip: A workbench can be equipped with useful accessories, like pegboard screwed to the bench ends for storing saw blades and small tools, or woodworking vises.

Lumber List: six 8-foot 2 × 4s, one 5-foot 2 × 6, one 4 × 8-foot sheet of ¾" plywood, one 4 × 8-foot sheet of ½" plywood, one 4 × 8-foot sheet of ⅛" hardboard. Use a framing square to mark pieces, and cut with circular saw to dimensions indicated below.

KEY	Pcs	SIZE AND DESCRIPTION
A	1	⅛-inch hardboard top, 24" × 60"
B	2	¾-inch plywood top, 24" × 60"
C	4	2 × 4 crosspieces, ends, 21"
D	4	2 × 4 legs, 19¾"
E	4	2 × 4 legs, 34½"
F	4	2 × 4 legs, 7¾"
G	3	2 × 4 braces, 54"
H	1	2 × 6 front (top) brace, 57"
I	1	½-inch plywood shelf, 14" × 57"
J	1	½-inch plywood shelf back, 19¼" × 57"
K	1	1 × 4 backstop, 57"

How to Build a Workbench

1 For each end, cut two each of pieces C, D, E, and F. Assemble with 2½-inch wallboard screws.

2 Attach both 2 × 4 rear braces (G, G) inside back legs of assembled ends. Use 2½-inch wallboard screws.

3 Attach 2 × 4 front lower brace (G) inside front legs of assembled ends. Secure bottom shelf (I) and workbench back (J) with 2½-inch wallboard screws to assembled 2 × 4 frame.

4 Drill pilot holes and join 2 × 6 front upper brace (H) outside front legs with 3-inch lag screws.

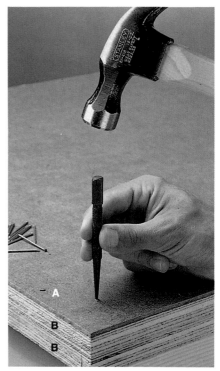

5 Center bottom layer of ¾-inch plywood work surface (B) on top of frame. Align with back edge, and hold in place with 4d nails.

6 Align bottom and top layers of plywood work surface (B, B). Drive 3-inch wallboard screws through both layers into bench frame.

7 Nail hardboard work surface covering (A) to plywood substrate (B, B) with 4d finish nails. Set nails below surface.

How to Mount a Tabletop Bench Vise

1 Position vise at end of bench. On bench top, mark holes in vise base. Bore ¼-inch holes into bench top to secure vise.

2 Attach vise with 1½-inch lag screws. Attach backstop (K) to back of bench top, with 2½-inch wallboard screws.

Sawhorses

Sawhorses are used to support work materials for marking and cutting. They can also form the base for sturdy temporary scaffolding to use while painting or installing wallboard. For scaffolding, place good-quality 2 × 10s or 2 × 12s across two heavy-duty sawhorses. Small break-down sawhorses are a good choice if storage space is limited.

Before You Start:
Tools & Materials: four 8-foot 2 × 4s, 2½-inch wallboard screws, circular saw, framing square, screwgun or cordless screwdriver.

Lumber Cutting List

KEY	Pcs	SIZE AND DESCRIPTION
A	2	Vertical braces, 2 × 4, 15½"
B	2	Top rails, 2 × 4, 48"
C	1	Bottom brace, 2 × 4, 48"
D	2	Horizontal braces, 2 × 4, 11¼"
E	4	Legs, 2 × 4, 26"

Easy-storing Sawhorses

Fold metal sawhorses and hang them on the workshop wall when they are not in use.

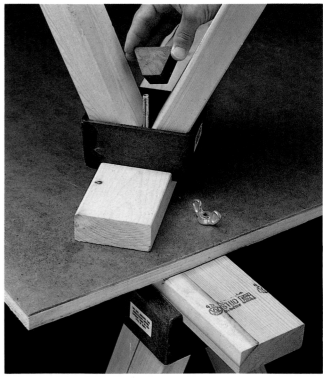

Buy brackets made from fiberglass or metal, and cut a 48-inch top rail and four 26-inch legs from 2 × 4s. Take sawhorses apart for storage.

How to Build a Heavy-duty Sawhorse

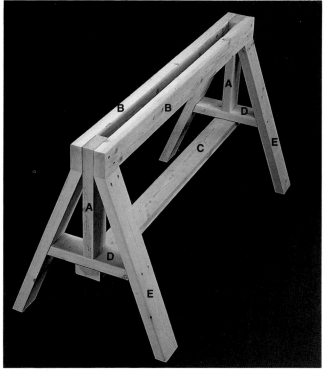

1 Heavy-duty sawhorse has wide top for supporting large loads. Cut vertical braces (A), top rails (B), and bottom brace (C) to lengths specified in Lumber Cutting List (page opposite).

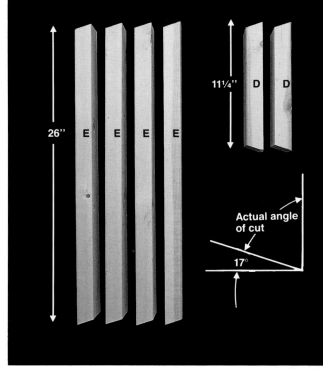

2 Set circular saw to 17° bevel angle. (Bevel cuts will match angle shown above.) Cut ends of horizontal braces (D) with opposing angles. Cut ends of legs (E) with parallel angles.

3 Attach top rails (B) to vertical braces (A), as shown, using 2½-inch wallboard screws.

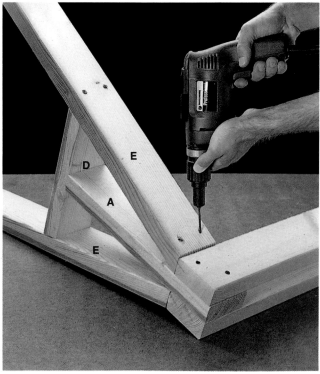

4 Attach horizontal braces (D) to vertical braces (A), using 2½-inch wallboard screws. Attach legs (E). To complete sawhorse, attach bottom brace (C) to horizontal braces (D).

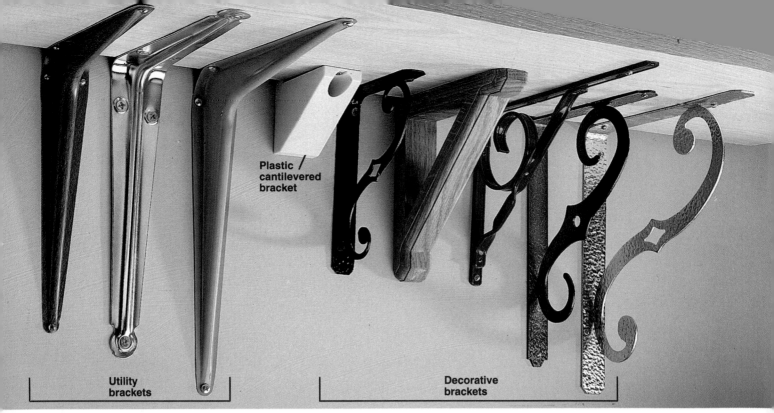

Plastic cantilevered bracket

Utility brackets

Decorative brackets

Stationary brackets are available in both decorative and utility styles, and come in a wide range of sizes. For greatest strength, choose brackets with diagonal supports. In most applications, attach longer bracket arm to the wall, and shorter arm to the shelf.

Ready-to-Hang Shelving

Shelves are sturdiest when their supports are anchored directly to wall studs. If brackets must be anchored between studs, use mollies or toggle bolts, and follow manufacturer's weight limits. On cement or brick walls, use masonry anchors to attach shelf supports.

Before You Start:
Tools & Materials: stud finder, shelving brackets, drill and bits, screwdriver, carpenter's level.

Tip: To minimize sagging on shelves, mount the brackets at least 6" from the ends of the shelves.

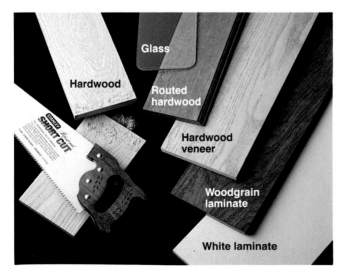

Glass

Hardwood

Routed hardwood

Hardwood veneer

Woodgrain laminate

White laminate

Shelves include: 1-inch hardwood cut to size, decorative glass, hardwood board with routed edge, hardwood veneer over processed wood, woodgrain plastic laminate over chipboard, and white plastic laminate.

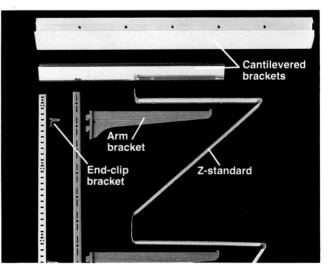

Cantilevered brackets

Arm bracket

End-clip bracket

Z-standard

Shelving standards include: horizontal cantilevered brackets, Z-standard for utility shelves, adjustable arm-bracket standard, adjustable end-clip standard.

How to Hang Shelf Brackets & Standards

Attach hardware to studs whenever possible. Use an electronic stud finder to locate studs (page 47). For heavy loads, attach a standard to every stud along span of shelf.

Molly bolts (shown) and toggle bolts expand and grip inside wallboard to support loads.

Molly bolt before tightening.

Molly bolt after tightening.

Attach hardware between studs using mollies or toggle bolts. Do not exceed manufacturer's recommended load limits for between-stud installation.

Attach hardware to masonry using plastic concrete anchors and screws (page 34). Attach one shelf bracket for every 16 to 24" of shelf span, depending on the intended load weight.

Level shelf brackets and standards using a carpenter's level. If necessary, hold the level on a straight 2 × 4 for leveling wide spans.

Simple Shelving

Sturdy wall shelving can be installed quickly using slotted metal standards and arm brackets. Use a stud finder to locate the wall studs, and attach the shelving standards directly to the studs for the greatest strength. Long wall shelves should be supported by standards every 48 inches.

For more decorative shelving, mortise the metal standards into strips of hardwood (above). Use an electric router to cut grooves into the hardwood strips, then insert the metal standards inside the grooves and attach them to the wall. A router can also be used to mold a decorative edge on the shelves.

Before You Start:

Tools & Materials: saw, 1 × 2 hardwood strips, 1 × 8 hardwood boards, router and straight bit, portable tool table, metal shelving standards, drill and bits, 3-inch wallboard screws.

How to Build & Hang Simple Shelving

1 Cut 1 × 8 hardwood shelves to chosen length. Cut 1 × 2 hardwood strips to same length as metal shelving standards. Position metal standards on hardwood strips, and trace outline on the wood.

2 Cut groove along center of each strip using a router and straight bit. Mount router in portable tool table for best control. Make several passes until groove is equal in depth and thickness to metal standard.

3 Insert standards into the routed grooves, then drill pilot holes through the hardwood strips at each screw opening.

4 Attach standards to wall studs with 3-inch wallboard screws. Use a carpenter's level to make sure standards are plumb and arm brackets will be level. Attach arm brackets and hang shelves.

Built-in Shelving

Permanent shelves can be built into any space where storage is needed. The space between a door or window and an adjacent wall corner is often used for built-in shelving.

A shelving unit can be built out of any 1-inch lumber except particleboard, which sags under heavy weight. For heavy loads, like books, a shelving unit should be built from 1 × 10- or 1 × 12-inch hardwood boards and should span no more than 48 inches. Shelves can be supported from the ends by pegs or end clips.

Before You Start:
Tools & Materials: tape measure, saw, framing square, 1 × 10- or 1 × 12-inch hardwood lumber, 2 × 2 lumber, scrap pegboard, drill and ¼-inch bit, paint or wood stain, hammer, 6d finish nails, 12d common nails, trim moldings, nail set.

Tip: When framing the basic shelving unit, build it 1" shorter than the floor-to-ceiling measurement. This allows you to tilt the unit into position without damaging the ceiling. Trim moldings are used to hide gaps along the ceiling and floor.

How to Construct a Built-in Shelving Unit

Cut baseboard

Cut baseboard

1 Measure the height and width of the available space. For easy installation, the basic unit is built 1" shorter than ceiling height. Remove baseboards (page 25), and cut them to fit around shelving unit. Replace baseboards after unit is nailed in place.

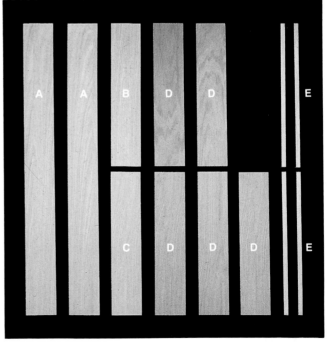

2 Mark and cut: two sides (A), 1" shorter than floor-to-ceiling measurement; unit top (B), bottom (C), and shelves (D), each 1½" shorter than unit width measurement; four 2 × 2 frame supports (E), 1½" shorter than unit width measurement.

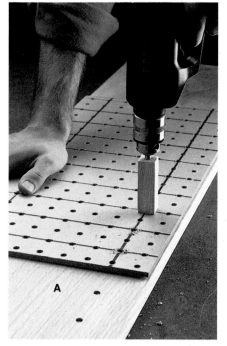

3 Using scrap pegboard as guide, drill pairs of ¼-inch holes along inside of each side (A), spaced horizontally 9" apart and vertically every 2". Holes should be ⅜" deep. Use scrap wood or bit attachment as depth guide.

4 Paint or stain wood as desired before assembling unit. Attach sides (A) to ends of frame supports (E). Drive 6d finish nails through sides and into end grain of frame supports.

5 Tilt unit into position flush against wall. Nail through top rear frame support (E) into wall studs, and through bottom frame supports into floor, using 12d common nails. Replace cut baseboards around bottom of shelving unit.

6 Attach bottom (C) and top (B) inside shelving unit. Drive 6d finish nails through sides (A) into end grain of top and bottom.

7 Miter-cut trim molding to fit around top and bottom of shelving unit (pages 106-109). Attach trim with 6d finish nails. Use nail set to recess nail heads.

Closet Organizers

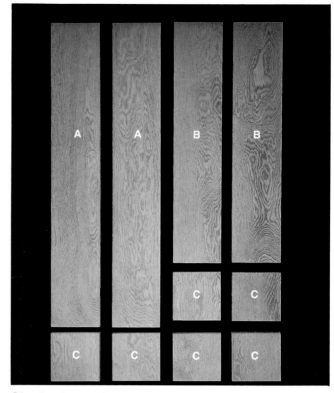

This organizer makes efficient use of space, and can double closet storage capacity. It may cost hundreds of dollars to buy custom-made organizers, but you can build an organizer for a 5-foot closet for the cost of a single sheet of plywood, a clothes pole, and a few feet of 1 × 3 lumber.

Before You Start:
Tools & Materials: hammer, finish nails (6d and 8d), 1 × 3 lumber, one 4 × 8-foot sheet of ¾-inch-thick plywood, tape measure, framing square, circular saw, clothes pole, six clothes-pole brackets, screwdriver, paint or wood stain.

Single sheet of plywood yields two 11⅞-inch-wide sides (A), two long 11⅞-inch-wide shelves (B), and six 11⅞-inch-square shelves.

How to Build a Closet Organizer

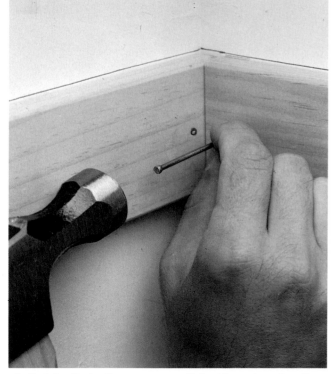

1 Cut 1 × 3 shelf supports to fit back and end walls of the closet. Attach supports to the wall with top edges 84" above floor, using 8d finish nails driven into the wall studs.

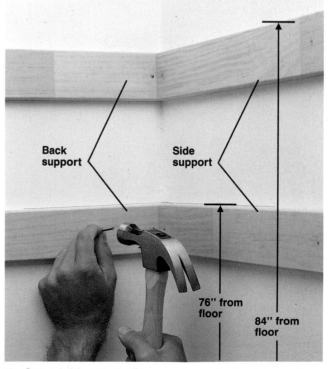

2 Cut additional shelf supports and attach to wall with top edges 76" above floor, using 8d finishing nails driven into wall studs.

(continued next page)

3 Cut two 11⅞-inch-wide shelves (B) from ¾-inch plywood. Cut length of shelves to fit closet width.

4 Measure and cut two 11⅞ × 76" shelf unit sides (A) from ¾-inch plywood.

5 Measure and cut six 11⅞-inch-square shelves (C) from ¾-inch plywood.

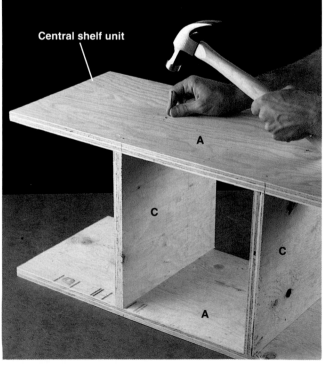

Central shelf unit

6 Assemble central shelf unit, using 6d finish nails. Space shelves evenly, or according to height of items stored. Leave top of unit open (see Step 8).

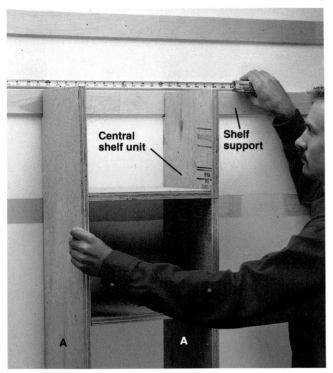

7 Position central shelf unit in middle of closet. Mark and notch shelf unit sides (A) to fit around lower shelf support.

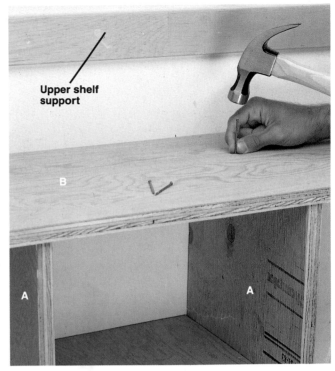

8 Lay long shelf (B) on lower shelf supports and top of central shelf unit sides (A). Attach with 6d finish nails. Lay remaining long shelf on upper shelf supports and attach with 6d finish nails.

9 Attach pole bracket to shelf unit side (A), 11" from rear wall and 3" below long shelf. Attach opposite bracket directly to wall stud with a screw or to wallboard using wall anchor (page 34). If desired, install brackets for lower clothes pole 38" above floor.

Finished closet organizer allows easy access to stored items. Place shoes, blankets, and other bulky articles in central shelf unit.

U-shaped brackets keep wood dry and permit air circulation so that lumber stays warp-free.

Utility Shelves

Building utility shelves is an easy way to organize a workshop, basement, garage, or attic. Use sturdy ladder-shaped brackets for support, and cut the shelves from ½- or ¾-inch plywood. Anchor utility shelving to the wall using wallboard screws or masonry anchors.

To store lumber in the basement or garage, build a hanging storage rack with U-shaped supports made from 1 × 4 lumber. The lumber rack keeps wood dry and flat, and can be suspended in the garage above the hood of your car to make efficient use of empty space.

Before You Start:
Tools & Materials for Utility Shelves: 2 × 2 lumber, tape measure, saw, carpenter's square, ⅜-inch-thick scrap plywood, carpenter's glue, wallboard screws (1- and 3-inch), screwgun or cordless screwdriver, ½- or ¾-inch-thick plywood.
Tools & Materials for Lumber Storage Rack: 1 × 4 lumber, tape measure, saw, metal connectors, 1-inch wallboard screws, screwgun or cordless screwdriver, drill and ¼-inch bit, 1½-inch lag screws.

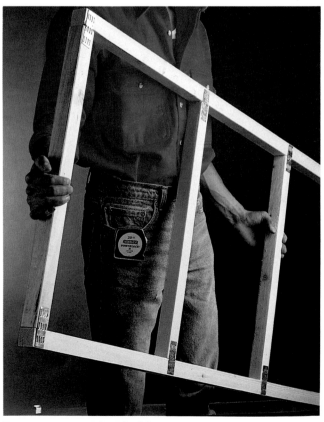

Buy preassembled ladder brackets for convenience when building utility shelves, or build brackets from 2 × 2 lumber (next page).

How to Build Utility Shelves

1 To build ladder brackets, cut the legs and cross braces from 2 × 2 lumber. Cross braces should be 3" shorter than width of shelves.

2 Assemble legs and cross braces with 4½-inch triangular gussets cut from ⅜-inch plywood, or metal connectors. Attach gussets with glue and 1-inch wallboard screws for strong joints.

3 Attach ladder brackets to wall studs, using 3-inch wallboard screws. If attaching to a concrete wall, use masonry anchors (page 34).

4 Cut shelves from ½- or ¾-inch plywood. Use a jig saw to cut 1½-inch square notches in shelves to fit around legs of ladder brackets.

How to Build a Lumber Storage Rack

1 Measure height, length and width of rack area. For garage storage, make sure rack will hang above level of car hood. Lumber storage rack requires one U-shaped support every 4'.

2 From 1 × 4 lumber, cut 2 legs and 1 cross brace for each U-shaped support. Cross brace should be 7" shorter than overall width of storage rack.

3 Assemble legs and cross braces with metal connectors and 1-inch wallboard screws.

4 Drill ¼-inch pilot holes through top of each leg and through ceiling joists. Attach supports to joists with 1½-inch lag screws. On finished ceilings, attach 2 × 4 ceiling plates to ceiling (page 84), then attach lumber rack supports to the ceiling plates.

Walls

Planning a Remodeling Job

Whether a remodeling job is simple or complex, start each project with a plan drawn to scale on graph paper. Use a large scale, like 1 inch = 1 foot, that is easy to read. From the plan, develop a list of tools and materials needed for the job. With this information, it is possible to compare prices between suppliers when estimating the cost of the project.

Check with local housing authorities before beginning a remodeling project. Changes that alter a home's structure require a building permit. Most changes to plumbing, heating or electrical systems require separate permits. If the job does require a permit, submit a scale drawing and materials list to the inspector along with the application. Make sure the job-in-progress is inspected as required by the building code.

Draw detailed plan using large scale, like 1 inch = 1 foot. Show all dimensions, wall openings, electrical and plumbing fixture locations. Indicate what materials will be used. Submit plan and materials list with permit application.

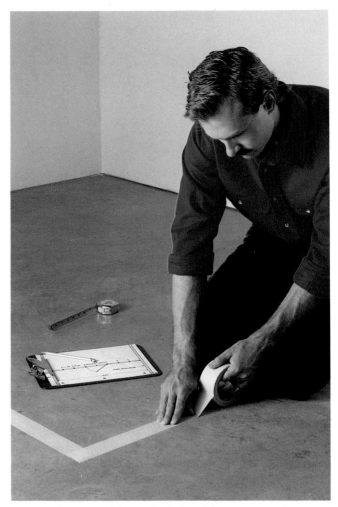

Lay project out. Use 2-inch masking tape on floor to show wall and door locations. Actual-size layout helps in visualizing the end result.

Common Remodeling Tools & Materials

Lumber: 1 × 2 furring strips, 2 × 2, 2 × 4, 2 × 6 framing lumber, wood shims, window and door case molding, baseboard molding, ¼-round shoe molding.

Plywood/Sheet goods: ½-inch wallboard (4 × 8-, 4 × 12-foot sheets), ⅜-inch wallboard, water-resistant wallboard, sheathing-grade plywood, finish plywood (½", ¾" thick), ¾-inch particleboard, wood paneling, foam insulating panels, fiberglass roll insulation, Sound Stop® board.

Fasteners: common nails (6d, 8d, 16d), finish nails (4d, 6d, 8d), concrete nails, wallboard screws (1½-, 2½-, 3-inch), lag screws, masonry anchors, Grip-It® wall anchors, metal connectors.

Adhesives: panel adhesive, construction adhesive, hot glue sticks, carpenter's glue.

Miscellaneous: prehung interior doors and windows, lockset, wallboard taping compound and tape, paint, wallcovering, electrical fixtures, lighting fixtures, plumbing fixtures, stepladders, sawhorses.

Hand tools: 16-ounce curved claw hammer, wallboard hammer, pry bar, screwdrivers (standard, phillips head), framing square, combination square, wallboard square, carpenter's level, T-bevel, clamps, ¾-inch steel tape measure, plumb bob/chalk line, electronic stud finder, carpenter's crayon, utility knife and blades, crosscut saw, backsaw and miter box, hacksaw, coping saw, block plane, wallboard knives (6-, 10-inch), mud pan, caulk gun.

Power tools: circular saw and blades, jig saw and blades, router and cutting bits, variable-speed drill and bits, screwgun or cordless screwdriver, electric sander and sandpaper, extension cord.

Extras: building permit, tool rentals, contractors for plumbing and electrical work.

Building & Finishing Interior Walls Step-By-Step (details on following pages)

1 Install the top plate. If you want to soundproof the walls, see pages 110-111 for variations on framing techniques.

2 Install the sole plate. Use a plumb bob to align the sole plate directly under the top plate.

3 Install the wall studs. Attach the studs with metal connectors, or by toenailing the joints.

4 Frame for a prehung door (pages 88-91). Prehung doors are already mounted in the jamb. Frame the door opening ⅜" larger on each side than the door unit.

5 Run any water pipes and wiring through framed wall. Protect mechanicals from nail or screw punctures by covering them with flat metal plates.

6 Install wallboard (pages 92-97). Use ½-inch wallboard for most applications or, install wood paneling (pages 102-105). Finish wallboard (pages 98-101).

7 Install prehung door (pages 114-115). Prehung doors come complete with jambs and mitered door casing.

8 Cut and install the door casings (pages 106-109). Stain or paint the trim pieces as desired.

Framing an Interior Wall

Interior walls usually do not bear weight, so they are easier to build than exterior, load-bearing walls. A simple interior wall is made from a horizontal top plate nailed to the ceiling, a sole plate attached to the floor directly under the top plate, and a series of parallel vertical studs spaced at 16- or 24-inch intervals.

Calculate the lumber needed to place a stud every 16 or 24 inches, as specified by local building code. Add the lumber needed for the top and sole plates, as well as for ceiling blocking (below). Include door framing materials, if needed.

Before You Start:
Tools & Materials: electronic stud finder, 2 × 4 lumber, tape measure, hammer, circular saw, plumb bob, combination square, common or box nails (4d, 6d, 8d and 16d), metal connectors, flat metal plates, caulk gun, construction adhesive, 8d hardened concrete nails.

Tip: For soundproofing interior walls see pages 110-111.

How to Frame an Interior Wall

1 Use stud finder to locate both edges of each ceiling joist. Mark position and direction of joists with pencil. If blocking has been installed, locate and mark edges of each blocking member.

Fastening New Wall to Existing Framing (shown with ceiling removed)

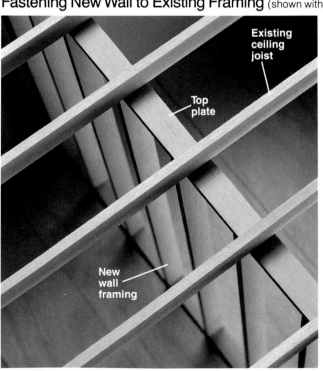

Nail top wall plate directly into the joists if the new wall runs perpendicular to the existing ceiling frame members.

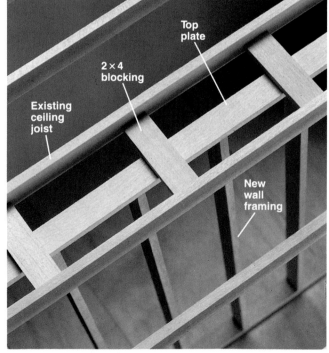

Install 2 × 4 blocking between joists if new wall is parallel to, but not under, joists. Attach blocking with 8d nails. Blocking provides anchoring surface for new wall. If ceiling joists are not accessible for blocking, install wall directly under joist.

2 Measuring from the existing wall, mark the location of the new wall top plate on the ceiling.

3 Cut the top and sole plates, then position them side by side. Mark stud locations at 16- or 24-inch intervals, as specified by local building code.

4 Use a combination square to outline location of studs. Make an "X" mark at each stud location. Mark one end of each plate for reference.

5 Hold top plate in position on ceiling, and attach it with 16d nails driven into the joists or blocking.

(continued next page)

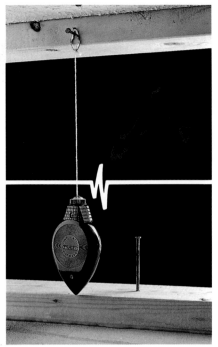

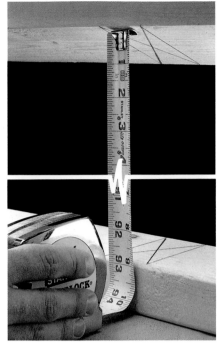

6 To position sole plate, hang plumb bob from edge of top plate so that tip nearly touches the floor. When plumb bob hangs motionless, mark position on floor. Take floor plumb markings from each end of top plate. Position sole plate against marks.

7 To attach sole plate to concrete, apply construction adhesive to bottom of plate and drive hardened concrete nails every 16". On wood floors, nail plate every 16" with 8d nails.

8 Measure distance between top and sole plates at each stud location. Cut each stud to measurement with circular saw. An uneven floor or ceiling causes stud lengths to vary slightly.

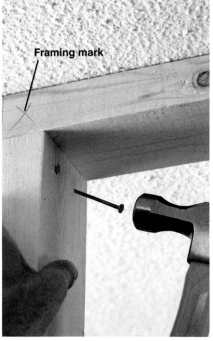

Framing mark

9 Drive studs into position with a hammer. Align each stud end with the framing marks on top and sole plates.

10 Attach studs to plates by nailing metal connectors over joints with 6d or 8d nails.

Nailing alternative: studs can be attached to plates with 6d or 8d nails toenailed through sides of studs at 45° angles.

How to Frame Corners (shown in cutaways)

L-corners: Nail 2 × 4 spacers (A) to inside of end stud. Nail an extra stud (B) to spacers. Extra stud provides a surface for nailing wallboard on inside corner.

T-corner meets stud: Fasten 2 × 2 backers (A) to each side of side wall stud (B). Backers provide nailing surface for wallboard.

T-corner between studs: Fasten a 1 × 6 backer (A) to end stud (B) with wallboard screws. Backer provides nailing surface for wallboard.

How to Run Pipes & Wiring through Framing

1 Drill holes in studs with power drill and spade bit or hole saw, as needed to run plumbing pipes, electrical or telephone wires.

2 Cover wire locations with flat metal plates nailed to studs. Plates protect wires and pipes from damage by wallboard screws or nails.

Top plate

Cripple
stud

Door
header

King stud

Jack stud

Sole
plate

Framing a Prehung Interior Door

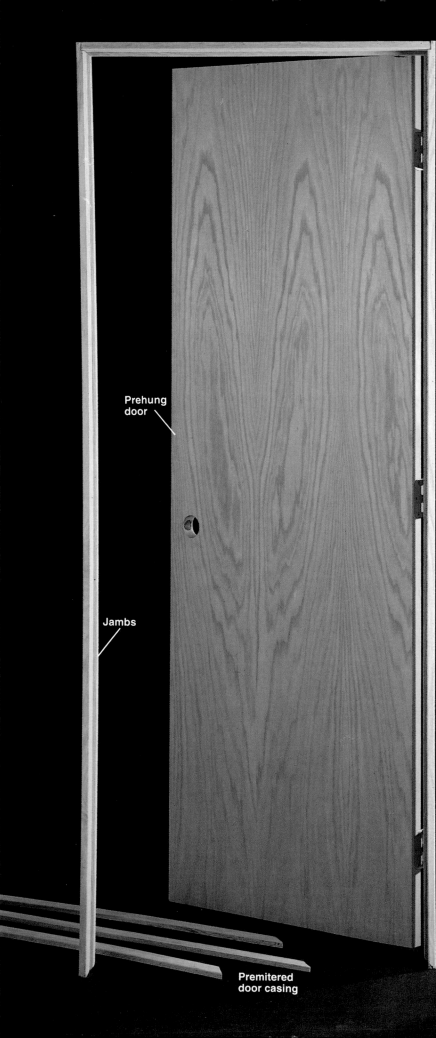

Prehung door

Jambs

Premitered door casing

Build door frames with straight, dry lumber so the door unit fits evenly into the rough opening. With good-quality lumber, the framing will not warp and cause the door to bind.

First buy the prehung door. Most interior doors are 32 inches wide, but narrower and wider styles are readily available. Next, calculate the size for the rough opening and install the door framing.

Most prehung doors are 82 inches high. Allow an extra ⅜ inch for clearance, so the unit can be adjusted for plumb and level inside the rough opening. Cut the jack studs 80⅞ inches long, and set the bottom of the header 82⅜ inches high. Note: Install door (pages 114-115) after wallboard is installed.

Before You Start:
Tools & Materials: prehung door unit, tape measure, 2 × 4 lumber, framing square, 8d common nails, metal connectors, handsaw.

89

How to Frame a Prehung Interior Door

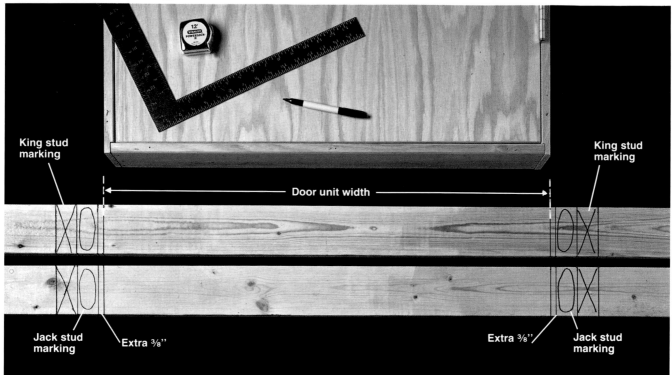

King stud marking

King stud marking

Door unit width

Jack stud marking   Extra ⅜"   Extra ⅜"   Jack stud marking

1 Position top of door frame next to top and sole plates, as shown. Measure width of door unit to outside edges of jambs. Mark the distance on top and sole plates. Measure an extra ⅜" on each side and mark plates again. Mark off 1½" stud markings for jack studs and king studs.

2 Install top plate and sole plate. Do not nail sole plate to floor between jack stud locations, because this portion of plate will be removed before door installation.

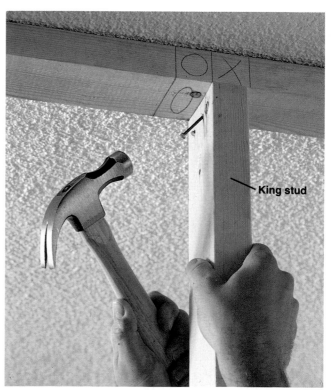

King stud

3 Measure and cut king studs and position at markings (X). Drive nails at 45° angle for toenailed joint, or attach studs with metal connectors (page 22).

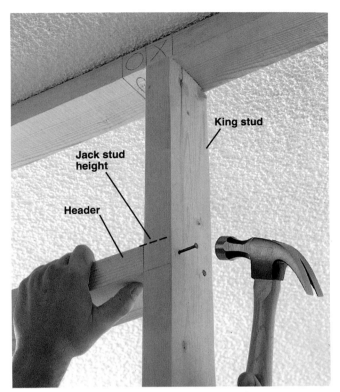

4 Mark height of jack stud on each king stud. Nail header to king stud above 82⅜-inch jack stud mark.

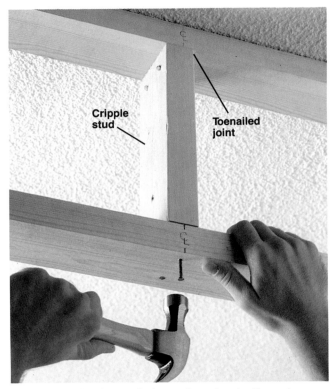

5 Install cripple stud above header, halfway between king studs. Toenail cripple stud to top plate, and nail through bottom of header into cripple stud.

6 Position jack studs against inside of king studs, and nail in place. Nail through top of header down into jack studs.

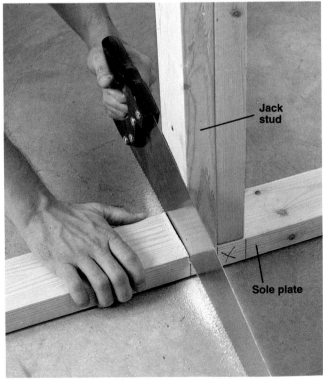

7 Saw through the 2 × 4 sole plate at inside edges of jack studs. Remove cut portion of plate.

Installing Wallboard

Wallboard is commonly available in 4 × 8- and 4 × 12-foot sheets, and in thicknesses ranging from ⅜ to ¾ inch. For easy handling in most applications, use 4 × 8-foot sheets of ½-inch-thick wallboard. For extra fire protection where building codes require it, or for soundproofing walls and ceilings, use ⅝-inch wallboard.

Install wallboard with wallboard nails and a wallboard hammer. Wallboard can also be installed with panel adhesive and wallboard screws. Adhesives bridge minor framing problems, and provide a smooth, easy-to-finish surface that is not subject to nail pops.

Wallboard panels are tapered along the long edges, so that adjoining panels form a slightly recessed seam that can be easily covered with paper tape and wallboard joint compound. Panels joined end-to-end are difficult to finish, so avoid end-butted seams wherever possible.

Before You Start:
Tools & Materials: straightedge, hammer, 4 × 8-foot wallboard panels, tape measure, wallboard T-square, utility knife, wallboard saw, jig saw, circle cutter, sawhorse scaffolding (page 60), wallboard hammer, wallboard nails, screwgun, 1¼-inch wallboard screws, wallboard lifter, panel adhesive, caulk gun.

Tip: Inspect wallboard panels for broken corners and cracks before installation. Damaged wallboard is difficult to install, and causes finishing problems.

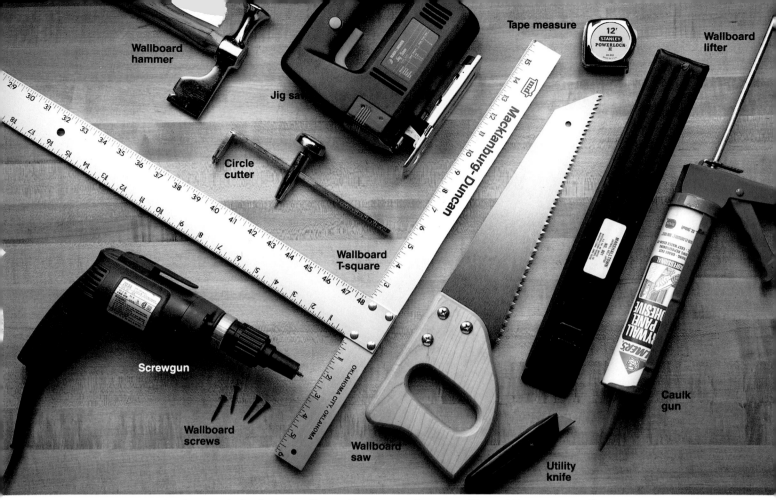

Wallboard installation tools include: wallboard hammer with convex head for indenting nail heads, jig saw, tape measure, wallboard lifter for positioning wallboard panels, caulk gun and panel adhesive, utility knife, wallboard saw for straight cuts around windows and doors, wallboard T-square, wallboard screws, screwgun with adjustable clutch for adjusting screw depth, circle cutter for making round cutouts for wall lighting fixtures.

How to Prepare for Wallboard Installation

1 Check stud alignment with straightedge that is at least 4' long. Remove and replace any warped studs.

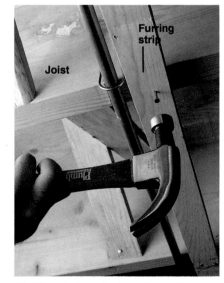

2 Check for obstructions, like water pipes or heating ducts that hang below joists. Nail furring strips to framing to extend wall surface, or move obstructions.

3 Mark locations of studs with carpenter's pencil or masking tape on floor. Wallboard will cover studs, so these marks show where to nail.

How to Cut Wallboard

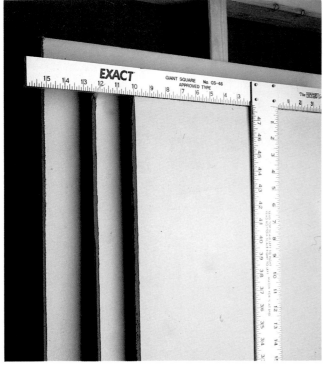

1 Set wallboard upright with smooth side out when cutting panels. Cut and install wallboard panels one at a time.

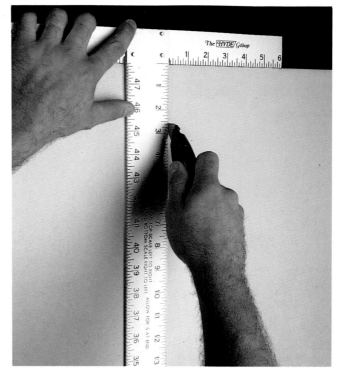

2 Use tape measure to measure length needed. Position wallboard T-square with short arm flush against edge. Use a utility knife to score wallboard face paper along long arm of square.

3 Bend scored section with both hands to break plaster core of wallboard. Fold back unwanted piece. Cut through back paper to separate pieces.

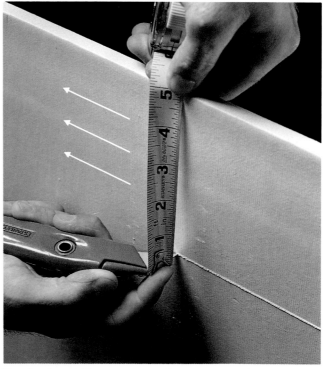

For horizontal cuts, extend tape measure to width of desired cut, and hook utility knife blade under end of tape. Hold tape tightly in one hand, utility knife tightly in other hand. Move both hands along panel to score a cut in face paper.

How to Cut Notches and Openings in Wallboard

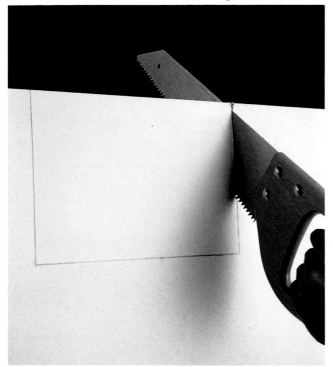

1 Use a wallboard saw to cut shortest sides of notch. A wallboard saw has coarse, wide-set teeth that cuts quickly without clogging.

2 Use a utility knife to cut remaining side of notch, then break plaster core as shown. Cut back paper with utility knife to separate unwanted portion.

Cut openings for electrical and telephone outlets, and heating ducts, by making plunge cuts with a jig saw and coarse, wood-cutting blade (page 17).

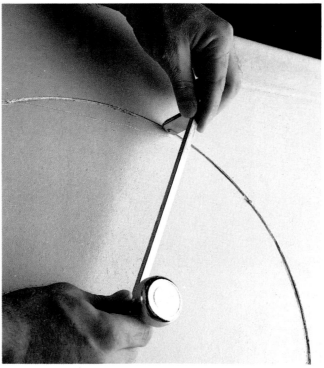

Make circular cutouts for light fixtures or exhaust fans with an adjustable circle cutter. Mark a center point and use the circle cutter to score both sides of wallboard. Tap with a hammer to release cutout from surrounding panel.

How to Install Wallboard Ceilings

1 Install wallboard panels on ceiling before installing wall panels. Mark ceiling joist locations on top plate as a nailing guide for installing wallboard. Always work with a partner when installing wallboard ceilings.

2 Place a sponge in work cap before installing wallboard on ceiling. Sponge provides cushion while worker uses head to hold panel in place for nailing.

3 Build a scaffold out of sawhorses and lumber (page 73) so the top of worker's head just touches bottom of ceiling joists. Use head to hold panel while it is nailed.

4 Apply panel adhesive to bottom of joists. Hold wallboard tightly against joists with top of head. This frees hands for nailing or screwing wallboard.

How to Install Wallboard Walls

1 Attach wallboard with panel adhesive and wallboard screws. Apply adhesive to studs with caulk gun. At joints, apply adhesive in a wavy pattern so both panel edges contact it.

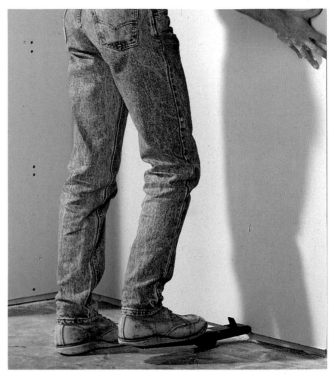

2 Install wallboard panels vertically to avoid butt joints that are difficult to finish. Lift panels tight against ceiling with wallboard lifter, then screw panels into position.

3 Drive 1¼-inch wallboard screws through panel into studs with screwgun. Follow screw interval recommended by manufacturer.

4 Plan wallboard placement so there are no joints at corners of doors or windows. Wallboard joints at corners often crack and cause bulges that interfere with miter joints in window or door trim.

Finishing Wallboard

To finish wallboard, apply wallboard compound to all seams, nail and screw holes, and corners. Because wallboard compound shrinks as it dries, three coats are needed to compensate for shrinkage. Apply the first coat with a 4- or 6-inch taping knife and let dry thoroughly. Apply the last two coats with a 10-inch knife.

To prevent cracking, all joints must be reinforced. On outside corners, nail metal corners over the wallboard before applying compound. On inside corners and flat joints, apply a thin first layer of compound, then press strips of paper wallboard tape into the damp compound.

Wallboard finishing tools include: plastic mud pan with metal edges for holding wallboard taping compound; wallboard wet sander for smoothing wallboard joints without raising dust; 4-, 6-, and 10-inch-wide wallboard knives; pole sander for sanding in high corners.

Tip: To avoid dust, use a wallboard wet sander instead of sandpaper to smooth joints.

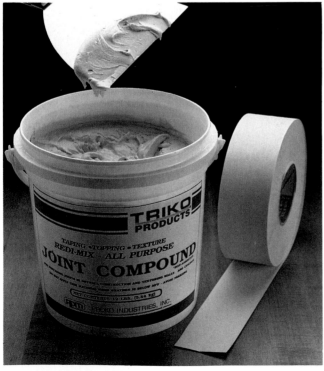

Use premixed wallboard compound for most taping and finishing jobs, to eliminate messy mixing. Use paper wallboard tape when using premixed wallboard compound.

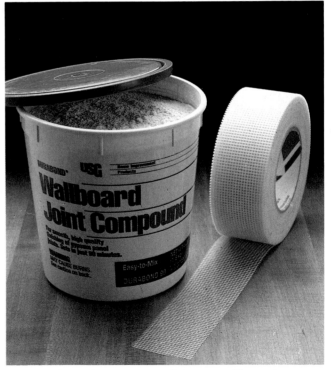

For small projects, use quick-set wallboard compound that is mixed with water. Quick-set compound hardens in 1 to 2 hours. Use fiberglass wallboard tape when using quick-set compound.

How to Tape Wallboard Joints

1 Apply a thin layer of wallboard compound over joint with a 4- or 6-inch wallboard knife. To load knife, dip it into mud pan filled with wallboard compound.

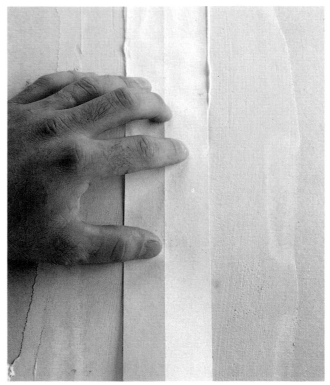

2 Press wallboard tape into compound immediately, centering tape on joint. Wipe away excess compound and smooth joint with 6-inch knife. Let dry.

3 Apply 2 thin finish coats of compound with 10-inch wallboard knife. Allow second coat to dry and shrink overnight before applying last coat. Let the last coat harden slightly before wet-sanding.

4 Smooth the finish coat with wallboard wet sander before compound dries completely. Wet sander smooths compound without raising plaster dust.

How to Finish Inside Corners

1 Fold a strip of paper wallboard tape in half by pinching the strip and pulling it between thumb and forefinger.

2 Apply thin layer of premixed wallboard compound to both sides of the inside corner, using a 4-inch wallboard knife.

3 Position end of folded tape strip at top of corner joint. Press tape into wet compound with wallboard knife, and smooth both sides of corner.

4 Apply second coat of compound to one side of corner at a time. When first side of corner is dry, finish opposite corner. After second coat dries, apply final coat of compound. Smooth final coat with wet sander (page 99).

How to Finish Outside Corners

1 Position steel corner bead on outside corners. Using a level, adjust bead so corner is plumb. Nail into place with 1¼-inch wallboard nails spaced at 8-inch intervals.

2 Cover corner bead with 3 coats of wallboard compound, using 6- or 10-inch wallboard knife. Let each coat dry and shrink overnight before applying next coat. Smooth final coat with wet sander (page 99).

How to Finish Nails & Screws

How to Sand Joints

Cover screw or nail heads with 3 coats of wallboard compound, using a 4- or 6-inch wallboard knife. Allow each coat to dry overnight before applying next coat.

Sand joints lightly after wallboard compound dries. Use pole sander to reach high areas without a ladder. Wear a dust mask when dry-sanding.

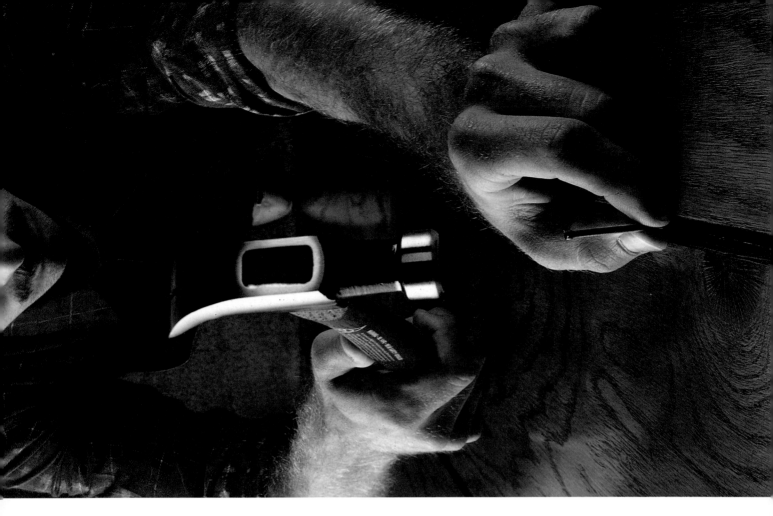

Installing Paneling

Paneling is a versatile wall-surfacing material that comes in a wide range of styles, colors, and prices. Wood paneling is a rich-looking alternative to paint or wallcovering, and is also used as an inexpensive cover-up for damaged plaster walls. It comes in 4 × 8-foot sheets, and is usually 3/16 or 1/4 inch thick. Paneling is available in both prefinished and un-finished sheets.

Paneling is durable and easy to clean, and is often used as wainscoting in a dining room or family room.

Before You Start:
Tools & Materials: pry bar, stud finder, tape measure, plumb bob, paneling sheets, circular saw, straightedge, hammer, 4d finish nails, carpenter's level, compass, jig saw, wood stain, caulk gun, panel adhesive, powdered chalk.

Tip: Room corners are often irregular. To fit paneling in corners that are not perfectly square, scribe the corner profile onto the first sheet of paneling with a compass. When marked profile is cut, paneling fits perfectly.

How to Cut & Fit Paneling

1 Remove all trim and molding from baseboards, windows, doors and ceilings. Use wood block under the pry bar to protect walls from damage.

2 Use an electronic stud finder to locate studs. Start in corner farthest from entry, and find stud that is closest to, but less than, 48" from corner. Find and mark studs every 48" from first marked stud.

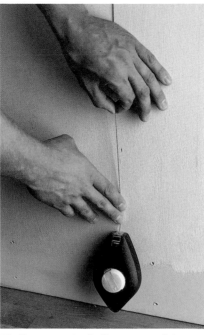

3 Snap a chalk line on wall to make plumb lines through stud marks. Paneling seams will fall along these lines.

Straightedge

4 Lay first paneling sheet face-side-down. Measure distance from corner to first plumb mark and add 1" to allow for scribing. Use a circular saw and clamped straight-edge to cut paneling to this measurement.

5 Position first sheet of paneling against wall so that cut edge is 1" away from corner, and opposite finished edge is plumb. Temporarily tack top of paneling to wall.

6 Spread legs of compass to 1¼". With point against wall corner and pencil against face of paneling, run compass down full height of wall. Corner irregularities are scribed on face of paneling. Remove paneling from wall.

7 Lay paneling face-side up, and cut along scribed line with jig saw. To prevent splintering, use a fine-tooth wood-cutting blade. Scribed edge fits perfectly against wall corner.

How to Install Paneling

1 Apply stain to wall at plumb line so the wall will not show through slight gaps at joints. Select a stain that matches color of paneling edges, which may be darker than paneling surface.

2 Use a caulk gun to apply 1-inch-long beads of panel adhesive to the wall at 6-inch intervals. Keep beads about 1″ back from plumb lines, to prevent adhesive from seeping out through joints. For new construction, apply adhesive directly to studs.

3 Attach paneling to top of wall, using 4d finishing nails driven every 16″. Press paneling against adhesive, then pull away from wall. Press paneling back against wall when adhesive is tacky, about 2 minutes.

4 Hang remaining paneling so that there is a slight space at the joints. This space allows paneling to expand in damp weather. Use a dime as a spacing gauge.

How to Cut Openings in Paneling

1 Measure window and door openings, and mark outlines of openings on back side of paneling.

2 Coat edges of electrical and telephone outlets and heating vents with chalk or lipstick.

3 Press back-side of paneling against wall. Marks on outlets and vents are transferred to paneling.

4 Lay paneling face-side-down. Drill pilot holes at one corner of each outline. Use a jig saw and fine-tooth woodcutting blade to make cutouts.

Cap

Crown (sprung cove)

Colonial baseboard

Chair rail

Ranch baseboard

Lattice

Colonial stop

Bifold door stop

Outside corner

Inside corner

Base shoe

Quarter-round

Trim & Molding

The most important tools for working with trim and moldings are a sharp pencil and a sharp saw in a quality miter box. These tools let you mark and cut miters accurately. Tight-fitting joints are the primary goal in trim carpentry, so you should buy or rent a quality miter box or power miter saw.

The basics of installing trim and moldings are shown here. With some practice, you can learn to combine two or more molding shapes to create custom moldings.

Before You Start:
Tools & Materials: sharp pencil, measuring tape, router with edging bits, miter box, coping saw, wood molding, finish nails, nail set.

How to Mold Your Own Trim

Miter box and back saw is used to cut precise angles on finish lumber, like mitered moldings for window and door casings.

How to Cut Miters in Moldings

Cut casings at 45° angle with flat edge tight against horizontal bottom base of the miter box. Baseboard miters are cut with molding tight against vertical rear base of miter box.

Cut sprung cove molding by positioning ceiling side of molding tight against horizontal bottom base of miter box. Wall side of molding should be tight against vertical rear base of miter box.

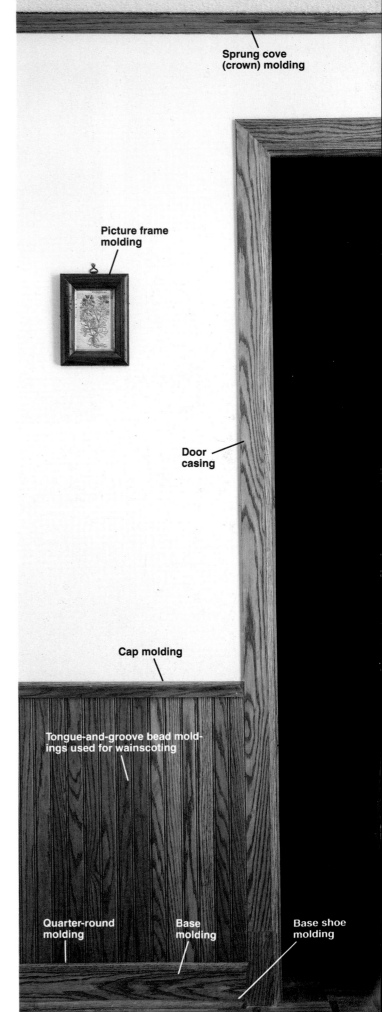

Sprung cove (crown) molding

Picture frame molding

Door casing

Cap molding

Tongue-and-groove bead moldings used for wainscoting

Quarter-round molding

Base molding

Base shoe molding

How to Cut & Fit Baseboards

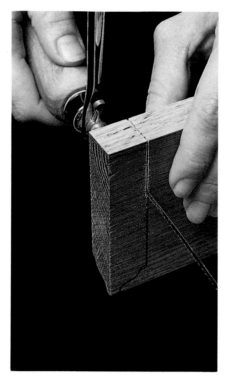

1 At inside corners, butt one end of baseboard into corner. On the backside of adjacent baseboard, outline the profile of baseboard with pencil.

2 With coping saw, trim baseboard along marked profile. Clamp baseboard in vise when cutting, and keep blade perpendicular to baseboard face.

3 Fit baseboard pieces in corner. Baseboard with coped edge fits tightly over adjoining square-cut baseboard molding.

4 Fit outside corners by cutting ends of baseboards at opposite 45° miters. Attach trim with finish nails, and recess nail heads (page 20).

5 For long spans, join shorter molding pieces by mitering the ends at parallel 45° angles. The mitered joint (scarf) cannot open up and show a crack if the wood shrinks.

How to Combine Moldings

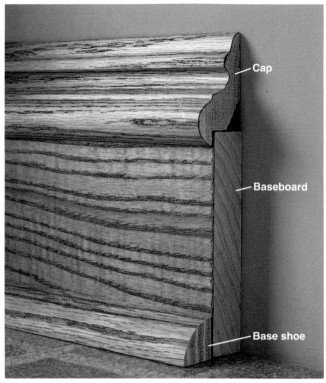

Pedestal base molding combines cap molding, flat baseboard, and base shoe molding. Nail moldings horizontally into framing members. Do not nail into flooring.

Decorative crown molding combines 2 sprung cove moldings. The square nailing strip in corner provides a nailing surface for both moldings.

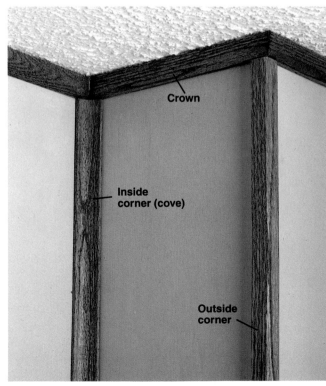

Inside and outside corner moldings add elegance to a room. Corner moldings on walls are often used with a cove or crown molding along the ceiling lines.

Cap molding is used to form a chair rail border on wainscoted walls.

New wallboard

2 × 4 framing

Old wallboard

Sound Stop board

Soundproofing Walls & Ceilings

The easiest way to soundproof is by using special materials and methods during construction, when framing is accessible. Your existing walls can also be soundproofed by adding materials like Sound Stop® board, or a layer of additional wallboard attached to resilient steel channels. These methods cushion the wall against noise transmission.

Walls and ceilings are rated for sound transmission by a system called Sound Transmission Class (STC). The higher the STC rating, the quieter the house. For example, if a wall is rated at 30 to 35 STC, loud speech can be understood through the wall. At 42 STC, loud speech is reduced to a murmur. At 50 STC, loud speech cannot be heard.

Standard construction methods result in a 32 STC rating, while soundproofed walls and ceilings can carry a rating of up to 48 STC.

Before You Start:
Tools & Materials for new walls: 2 × 6 top and sole plates, fiberglass batt insulation.
Tools & Materials for existing walls: Sound Stop® board, resilient steel channels, 5⁄8-inch-thick wallboard.

Tip: When building new walls, caulk along the floor and ceiling joints to reduce sound transmission.

Standard & Soundproofed Floor & Ceiling Construction

Standard construction, with plywood over wooden subfloor and ½-inch-thick wallboard on ceiling, carries a sound transmission rating of 32 STC.

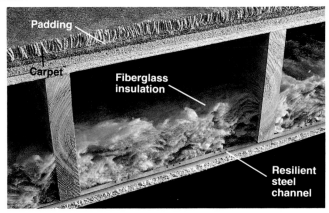

Padding
Carpet
Fiberglass insulation
Resilient steel channel

Soundproofed construction uses carpeting and padding on floor, fiberglass batt insulation, resilient steel channel nailed to joists, and ⅝-inch wallboard on ceiling. Rating for this system is 48 STC.

How to Soundproof New Walls

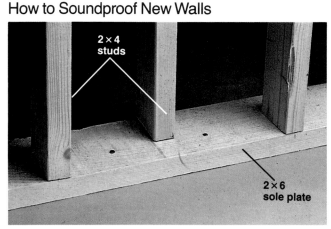

2 × 4 studs
2 × 6 sole plate

1 Build walls with 2 × 6 top and sole plates. Position 2 × 4 studs every 12", staggering them against alternate edges of plates.

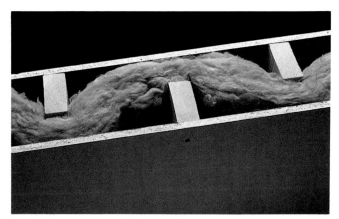

2 Weave 3½-inch unfaced fiberglass batt insulation between 2 × 4 studs throughout wall. When covered with ½-inch-thick wallboard, this wall has rating of 48 STC.

How to Soundproof Existing Walls & Ceilings

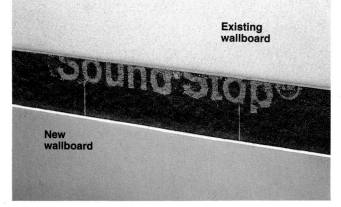

Existing wallboard
Sound Stop®
New wallboard

Nail ½-inch Sound Stop® board over existing surface with 1½-inch wallboard nails. Glue ½-inch-thick wallboard over Sound Stop with construction adhesive. Sound rating is 46 STC.

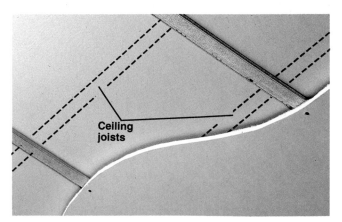

Ceiling joists

Screw resilient steel channels over ceiling or wall, spaced 24" on-center, perpendicular to existing framing. Attach ⅝-inch-thick wallboard to channels with 1-inch wallboard screws. Sound rating is 44 STC.

Doors

Installing Prehung Interior Doors

A prehung door unit includes the door, the door jamb, and premitered trim pieces. The hinges are already mortised and attached, and holes are bored for the lock and bolt. The job of installing the door is reduced to two tasks: positioning it plumb and square in the framed opening, and securing it with shims and nails so it swings properly.

Before You Start:
Tools & Materials: Wonderbar®, carpenter's level, cedar wood shims, hammer, finish nails (4d and 6d), nail set, saw.

Tip: If unit is to be finished, paint or stain door and trim before installing the unit.

How to Install a Prehung Interior Door

1 Remove shipping carton. Inspect unit for damage. Door has casing attached to one side of unit, and is packed with premitered casing for other side of door.

4 Gaps between jamb and framing at hinge and lock locations should be filled with shim material. Nail jamb to frame with 6d finish nails driven through shims.

2 Set door unit into framed opening. Check it for plumb with a carpenter's level.

3 To plumb door unit, insert wood shims between door jamb and frame on hinged side of door. Tap shims with hammer until level shows jamb is plumb.

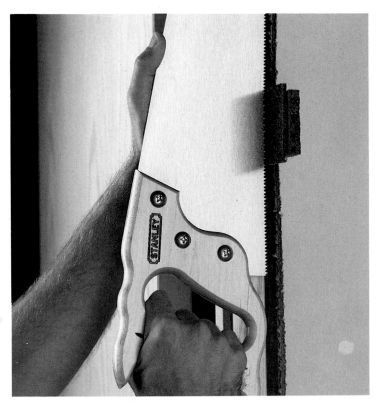

5 Cut off shims with handsaw. Hold saw vertically to avoid damaging the door jamb or wall.

6 Nail premitered trim to jambs, using 4d finish nails driven at 16-inch intervals. Recess nailheads with nail set (page 20).

Cutting Off an Interior Door

Prehung interior doors are sized to allow a ¾-inch gap between the bottom of the door and the floor. This gap lets the door swing without binding on the carpet or floorcovering. If thicker carpeting or a larger threshold is installed, a small portion of the door may need to be cut off with a circular saw.

Wider cuts may be needed if a door is altered to fit a special installation, like in a child's room or an undersized storage closet.

Hollow-core interior doors have a solid wood frame, with centers that are hollow. If the entire bottom frame member is cut away when shortening the door, it can be reinserted to close the hollow door cavity.

Before You Start:
Tools & Materials: tape measure, hammer, screwdriver, utility knife, sawhorses, circular saw and straightedge, chisel, carpenter's glue, clamps.

Tip: Measure carefully when marking a door for cutting. Measure from the top of the carpeting, not from the floor.

How to Cut Off an Interior Door

1 With door in place, measure ⅜" up from top of floorcovering and mark door. Remove door from the hinges by removing the hinge pins.

2 Mark cutting line. Cut through door veneer with sharp utility knife to prevent it from chipping when the door is sawed.

3 Lay door on sawhorses. Clamp a straightedge to the door as a cutting guide.

4 Saw off bottom of the door. The hollow core of the door may be exposed.

5 To replace a cut-off frame in the bottom of the door, chisel the veneer from both sides of the removed portion.

6 Apply wood glue to cut-off frame. Insert frame into opening, and clamp. Wipe away excess glue and let dry overnight.

Installing a Security Lock

How to Install a Security Lock

Security locks have long bolts that extend into the door jamb. They are also called deadbolts. The bolt of a security lock is moved in and out by a keyed mechanism.

Security locks help stop possible break-ins. Often home insurance rates can be lowered with the installation of security locks on exterior doors.

Before You Start:

Tools & Materials: tape measure, security lock (deadbolt), lockset drill kit (including hole saw and spade bit), drill, chisel.

Tip: A double-cylinder deadbolt lock has a key on both sides, and is the best choice for doors that have windows. Knob-type deadbolts can be opened by reaching through broken glass.

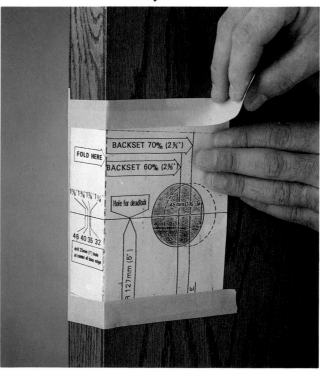

1 Measure to find lock location. Tape cardboard template, supplied with lockset, onto door. Use a nail or awl to mark centerpoints of cylinder and latchbolt holes on door.

2 Bore cylinder hole with a hole saw and drill. To avoid splintering door, drill through one side until hole saw pilot (mandrel) just comes out other side. Remove hole saw, then complete hole from opposite side of door.

3 Use a spade bit and drill to bore latchbolt hole from edge of door into the cylinder hole. Make sure to keep drill perpendicular to door edge while drilling.

4 Insert latchbolt into edge hole. Insert lock tailpiece and connecting screws through the latchbolt mechanism, and screw the cylinders together. Close door to find point where latchbolt meets door jamb.

5 Cut a mortise for strike plate with a chisel (pages 42-43). Bore latchbolt hole in center of mortise with spade bit. Install strike plate, using retaining screws provided with lockset.

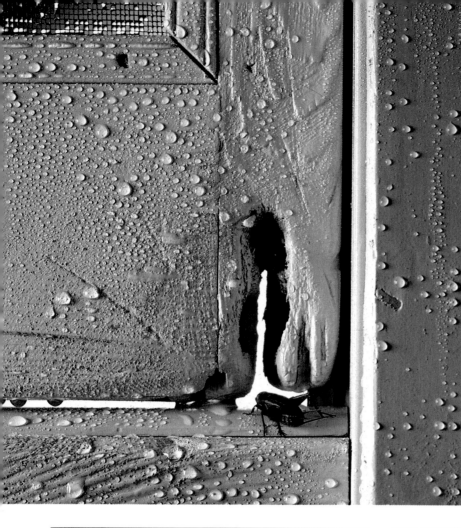

Preserving & Repairing Wood

Even durable woods like redwood or cedar benefit from a protective coat of sealer, stain or paint. Periodically inspect exterior doors, window sashes and decks so that rot or insect damage can be stopped before it becomes widespread. Seal joints around windows and doors with caulk to block entry by moisture or insects.

To repair existing wood damage, use one of the epoxy wood fillers available. Wood fillers can be molded and shaped easily, and they readily accept paint or stain.

Before You Start:
Tools & Materials: chisel, eye protection, wood filler, putty knives, sander, wood strips, tacks, tack hammer.

Protect wood exposed to weather with a clear or pigmented sealer. Treat wood yearly for best protection.

Repair damaged or rotted wood with epoxy wood filler (page opposite).

How to Repair Damaged Wood

1 Remove damaged wood with a chisel or utility knife. Wear eye protection while chiseling wood.

2 Build simple wooden forms as needed to establish repair boundaries. Coat forms with wax or oil so filler will not adhere to them.

3 Mix and apply wood filler according to directions. Shape repair area with putty knife or trowel to match existing contours. Let filler harden completely.

4 Remove forms. Sand hardened filler lightly — oversanding closes filler pores and makes staining difficult. Paint or stain the wood to match the existing finish.

Removing & Replacing an Entry Door

Replacing a warped, leaky entry door is a relatively easy project. New, energy-efficient entry doors come prehung with jambs and all installation hardware, except locks. Steel replacement doors will not warp or peel, are fully insulated and weatherstripped, and are more secure than wooden doors.

Before You Start:
Tools & Materials: tape measure, hammer, screwdriver, Wonderbar®, utility knife, silicone caulk, caulk gun, wood shims, carpenter's level, 16d galvanized nails, door lockset.

How to Remove & Replace an Entry Door

1 Measure height and width of existing door. Purchase replacement door to match measurements. Drive out hinge pins with hammer and screwdriver. Remove door.

2 Use a pry bar and hammer to gently remove interior door trim. Save trim to reapply after new door is installed.

3 Use a utility knife to cut away old caulk between the exterior siding and the brick molding on the door frame.

Brick molding

4 Pry away and discard old door jamb and threshold. Stubborn nails can be cut with a reciprocating saw.

(continued next page)

5 Place door unit into rough opening and check fit. There should be about ⅜-inch space on sides and top. Remove door unit.

6 Apply caulk to new threshold to form weather seal between the threshold and floor. Place door unit in rough opening.

7 Tap wood shims (filler strips) into gaps between frame and jambs until level shows unit is plumb. Insert shims at lockset and all hinge locations.

8 Nail through jambs and shims into framing members with 16d casing nails. Check for plumb after driving each nail.

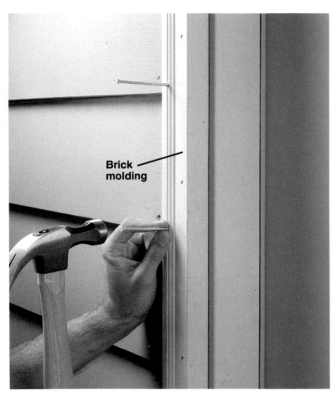

9 Drive 16d galvanized casing nails through brick molding into door frame.

10 Replace casing on inside of door jamb. If trim was damaged during removal, cut and install new casing.

11 Install new door lock. First, insert the latchbolt mechanism through latchbolt hole. Then insert the lockset tailpieces through latchbolt, and screw the handles together by tightening retaining screws.

12 Screw the strike plate to the door jamb and adjust the plate position to fit the latchbolt. Caulk any gaps between siding and new door molding.

Index

Cy DeCosse Incorporated offers a variety of how-to books. For information write:
Cy DeCosse Subscriber Books
5900 Green Oak Drive
Minnetonka, MN 55343